BUILT TO LAST
IN DIRECT
SELLING

THE SYSTEMS, CULTURE, AND LEADERSHIP FRAMEWORKS THAT COMBINE OLD-SCHOOL PRINCIPLES WITH MODERN-DAY EXECUTION

BY: ROB SPERRY

BUILT TO LAST
IN DIRECT
SELLING

THE SYSTEMS, CULTURE, AND LEADERSHIP FRAMEWORKS THAT COMBINE OLD-SCHOOL PRINCIPLES WITH MODERN-DAY EXECUTION

BY: ROB SPERRY

TGON Publishing

TGON Publishing

CONTENTS

INTRODUCTION
The Trust Recession   11

APPENDIX

The Momentum Sustainability Test

Will Your Company Still Be Growing in 5 to 10 Years?

This profession was never supposed to be about hype, shortcuts, or chasing stars. It was always about people — about belief, duplication, and building something that lasts.

This book became necessary the day a corporate exec pulled me aside and said, "I feel like I'm flying blind. The field's talking a different language. I don't know what they actually need, and I don't think they trust us."

THE TRUST RECESSION

That moment hit differently.

Not because it was rare, but because I'd already heard versions of it over and over. From the owners. Presidents. Heads of sales. Good people who want to lead well, but keep missing the mark.

They aren't the problem. The gap is.

The disconnect between corporate vision and field execution has become the quiet killer of momentum in direct sales. It shows up in the culture. It shows up in the data. And it shows up when companies start losing their best leaders and can't figure out why.

That's why this book exists.

It's not a warm welcome to the profession. It's not a highlight reel of inspiration. It's a reality check built from two decades of front-row access to the field and behind-the-scenes consulting with corporate teams.

If you want your company to last, you need to see what the best ones are doing differently—and what the struggling ones keep repeating.

This is the blueprint.

Your top leaders are scrolling Instagram at 11 PM, watching highlight reels from other companies' conventions. They're seeing the stage time, the recognition trips, the energy that screams "we're exploding with momentum", and they're starting to wonder: "Am I settling? Could I be making more somewhere else?"

That wandering eye? It's the first symptom of a trust recession that's quietly undermining network marketing companies from the inside out.

The Trust Recession in Direct Sales

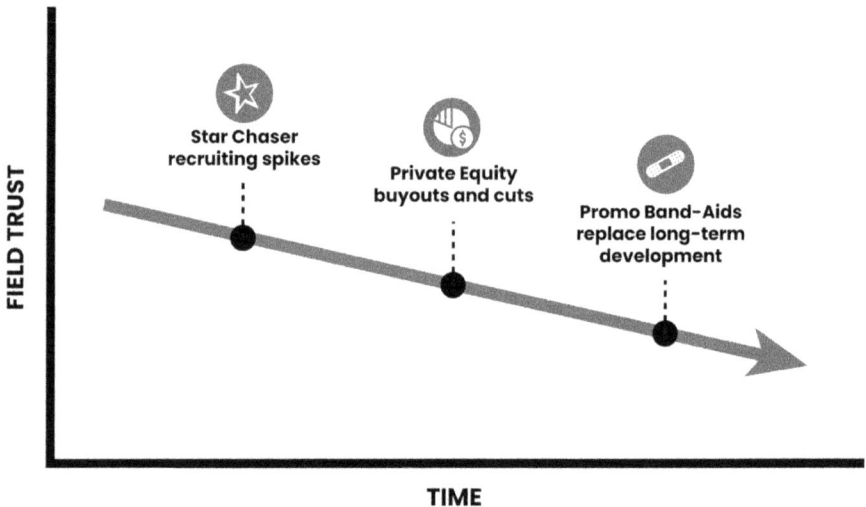

Trust erodes long before the volume does.

I've spent the last decade building at the top, consulted companies at the corporate level, and led over 30 elite masterminds exclusively for six and seven-figure earners. I run private groups with 1,700+ verified top earners who openly share real-time wins, breakdowns, and what's working across the industry. These aren't surface-level updates. These are unfiltered insights from the front lines—gathered daily from the people driving the profession forward.

And here's what I'm seeing: Trust is the most valuable currency in network marketing—and we're in a recession.

Not just field-to-corporate. Not just owner-to-leader. Everywhere. In an AI world full of filters, facades, and fast content, people have learned to question everything. And with good reason; we've trained them to.

In a relationship-driven profession, that's a problem you can't ignore. But most do—until the exits start happening.

Johnson & Johnson Proved What Real Trust Looks Like Under Fire

Johnson & Johnson gets blindsided: seven people die after taking cyanide-laced Tylenol in Chicago. The company's market share plummets from 35% to 8% almost overnight. Panic, lawsuits, and media chaos.

Most companies would have lawyered up and gone silent. J&J does the opposite—they pull 31 million bottles from shelves, halt all advertising, and open the doors to the press. They invent tamper-proof packaging and relaunch Tylenol within weeks, eating a $100 million loss.

The payoff? Tylenol's market share rebounds to 30% within a year, and J&J's reputation for transparency becomes the gold standard.

In direct sales, it means owning your mistakes and rebuilding from the ground up, not just spinning a new story.

Wells Fargo proved that when you reward the wrong behaviors, culture dies from the top down. But culture problems don't always start in the boardroom. Sometimes they start when corporate stops listening to what the field actually needs.

Nu Skin: How One Demo Rebuilt Belief

From 2001 to 2006, Nu Skin's North American sales dropped from $233.2 million to $212.6 million. At one point in 2004, they bottomed out at $198.7 million. Year after year, the numbers slipped. Quietly. Consistently. Painfully.

Meanwhile, international markets were exploding. Field leaders in the U.S. were watching recognition trips, hearing about surges in Asia, and wondering what went wrong. Some of the top earners stopped building in North America altogether. They shifted focus overseas, chasing the energy they couldn't create here anymore.

It wasn't just about the paychecks. It was about belief, and belief was gone.

Then something started bubbling up in Europe. Teams were leading with the Galvanic Spa—an old product most in North America had forgotten about. But instead of trying to explain the science, they were showing it. Five-minute demos. Simple. Physical. Real. You could see and feel it working on the spot.

The success was obvious, and it was duplicating.

So in 2007, Nu Skin brought that strategy home. They rolled out kits. They trained the field to run demos instead of lectures. Coffee shops turned into demo sessions. Living rooms turned into belief builders.

By 2008, sales jumped to $262.0 million. That was a 19% increase in one year.

Not from hype. Not from launching something new. Just from listening and returning to something simple that worked.

They didn't invent a new story. The field showed them what worked. Corporate just listened, bought in, and had the courage to change course—even scrapping planned product launches to focus on what was actually building belief.

That's the whole point. When you stop trying to sound smart and start helping your people feel confident, everything changes. This wasn't about breakthrough science. It was about field duplication, and duplication always wins.

The best leaders don't just say they listen to the field—they prove it by abandoning their own agendas when the field finds a better way. Nu Skin's North American turnaround didn't happen because corporate had the right strategy. It happened because they had the humility to follow the field's lead.

Nu Skin proved something crucial: culture isn't what you say in meetings—it's what you do when your field shows you what actually works. But they also proved how quickly you can lose that magic when you stop listening and start chasing complexity.

Most companies either try to control culture completely or abandon it entirely to the field. Both approaches fail. Control kills authenticity. Abandonment creates chaos. Smart companies create the framework, then let the field fill it with life.

What You Say About the Field—Even in Private—Shapes the Culture

Nu Skin proved that culture is built when corporate respects what the field knows. But culture is destroyed just as easily when corporate forgets that respect extends to private conversations.

Want to know how culture breaks? It doesn't start in public. It starts in side comments. In boardrooms. In back-office chats where someone jokes that the field is "entitled" or "lazy" or "just not getting it."

Even when it's said casually, it spreads and it's deadly.

We're not saying you can't be honest. You can and should have hard conversations. But you have to lead with respect—always. Because when corporate talks about the field like they're the problem, that mindset seeps into decisions, and eventually, it leaks into the field.

Culture is built top-down. When corporate rolls its eyes at distributor complaints, the rest of the company learns to do the same. When leaders privately criticize the field, they're not just venting. They're shaping how the entire organization views its most important asset.

Distributors are not always right. But they're always watching, and if they sense disrespect from corporate—even subtle, even unspoken—they'll pull back. Energy will fade. Communication will stall. Trust will collapse.

You don't have to fake it. But you do need to build a standard:

- No badmouthing the field—even behind closed doors

- Disagreements are handled with solutions, not sarcasm

- Leadership language stays professional, even when emotions run high

If you want the field to act like professionals, model it.

Awareness Is Everything—Because Blind Spots Don't Stay Small

Most companies don't implode from one bad decision. They erode quietly while everyone's clapping.

Some are bleeding culture, customers, and credibility without even realizing it; watching their best leaders quietly plan exits while they celebrate quarterly wins. Others are run by quick-fix executives who spike short-term numbers with gimmick promos, slap campaigns over cultural rot, and mistake motion for progress.

The best leaders I know aren't always the loudest. But they see clearly. They know where they're at. They know where the profession is going, and they're willing to make hard decisions before the pain forces it.

Too many companies say they want legacy but build like they need a win by Friday.

The launch looks good. The systems don't exist.

And the worst part? Everyone knows.

The field sees through it. The leaders talk. The numbers don't lie.

What This Book Will Give You

I've sat with owners who had momentum and didn't know it. I've talked to leaders who looked successful but were planning their exit. I've worked behind the scenes when companies were breaking—and helped rebuild them stronger.

I'm not guessing. I'm not theorizing. I'm the bridge between corporate and the field—and this book is what both sides need to hear before it's too late.

By the time you finish reading this, you'll know exactly why some billion-dollar companies collapsed while others thrived. You'll have the frameworks to diagnose your own vulnerabilities before they become fatal. You'll understand the difference between building for quarters and building for decades, and you'll have a roadmap for creating the kind of trust that turns wandering eyes into unwavering loyalty.

The field doesn't need you to have all the answers during a crisis. They need to know someone is steering the ship. Silence creates panic. Presence creates confidence. Even bad news delivered directly builds more trust than good news they have to guess about.

Field leaders follow people, not logos. When times get tough, they're not looking at your comp plan or your product line. They're looking for the human being who's going to lead them through it.

This isn't a motivational book. It's a mirror.

You'll see the things you've done right. You'll see what's working. You'll also see what's bleeding out—if you're honest enough to admit it.

This is for the brands that want to be around in 5, 10, 15 years—the ones willing to fight back against private equity vultures, star hunting executives, and quick-fix executives who are undermining everything we have built. It's for the founders who still care more about people than just P&L. It's for the field leaders who are done faking belief and ready to rebuild it.

Stop chasing perfection. Start leading with presence.

Your leaders are watching. Your competition is recruiting. The trust recession is real.

And every company that ignores these warning signs watches their momentum die while blaming the field.

The Three Enemies Destroying Network Marketing

PE VULTURES	STAR CHASERS	QUICK-FIX EXECUTIVES
Leverage companies with debt	Recruit with million-dollar deals	Slap promos over real problem
Cut field support for margins	Create expensive revolving doors	Chase quarterly wins
3-7 year exit timeline	Skip leadership development	Mistake motion for progress
Extract profits, not build culture	Buy talent instead of building	Spike numbers, ignore foundation

Legacy companies fight all three. Failing companies feed them.

The first place trust breaks? Leadership. Because when leaders go silent, people assume the worst, and in a profession where belief drives everything, the biggest leadership failure isn't executive misalignment—it's absence.

The biggest leadership failure

isn't executive misalignment.

It's absence.

CHAPTER 1

LEADERSHIP PRESENCE

The moment belief starts to fade, people don't just lose confidence in the business—they lose confidence in the leadership.

And when that happens, they don't always say it out loud. Sometimes they don't even realize it. But deep down, something shifts.

Momentum slows. Retention slips. Quiet questions start forming: "Who's steering this thing?"

Trust breaks long before the team walks away.

When belief starts to fade, people don't just lose confidence in the business-they lose confidence in the leadership.

Primerica Proved That Presence Beats Perfection When Everything Falls Apart

By 2008, Primerica was a direct sales powerhouse—millions of customers, $450 billion of life insurance in force, and 100,000+ licensed representatives. Then the financial world collapsed. Citigroup, Primerica's parent company, was imploding. AIG vanished. Lehman Brothers died overnight.

This wasn't just a market downturn—this was an existential crisis. Field representatives were terrified Primerica would be sold off or shut down. Their net worth had evaporated with Citi stock. Competitors were laying off thousands of reps and going silent.

But Co-CEOs Rick Williams and John Addison didn't retreat to boardrooms. Addison traveled to New York for what he called his "Moses meeting" with Citigroup's CEO—"Let my people go." Then he hit the road. While other executives hid behind lawyers and PR firms, Addison was visiting local meetings, sitting in living rooms with field leaders, and showing up at regional rallies across the country.

He didn't sugarcoat the crisis. Addison was known for his straight talk. He had learned early in his career that honesty, even when painful, built more trust than spin ever could. But he stayed present through it all. "I grew up with the company," Addison said. "I loved the organization and I knew the people."

His philosophy was simple: "Be a lighthouse, not a weathervane." While the industry panicked, Addison stayed visible, honest, and grounded. He believed a leader's job was to "have genuine care about the organization they're in charge of"—and that meant being out in the field, not watching from a distance.

The result? By 2010, Primerica went public in one of the most successful IPOs of the decade—22 times oversubscribed. The field didn't just survive the worst financial crisis in history—they grew stronger. Today, Primerica has grown from $1B to $9B market cap in 15 years.

For direct selling, this is the leadership playbook: When everything's falling apart, your field doesn't need spin or silence. They need to see you steering through the storm.

Presence doesn't solve everything. But it solves more than silence ever will.

In network marketing-a business built on emotion, trust, and community-it matters even more than it does in traditional companies.

This isn't a transactional model. It's a relationship-driven ecosystem. When the relationship with leadership gets quiet, the belief system breaks.

In an Era Where People Question Everything, Leadership Absence Feels Like Abandonment

Belief didn't die overnight. It leaked-slowly and quietly.

Enrollment stalled. Retention dipped. Your best leaders started taking calls from competitors. By the time you noticed, the damage was already done.

Not because the product failed—but because leadership disappeared.

This profession doesn't run on hierarchy. It runs on presence. In an era where people question everything, leadership absence feels like abandonment. You lead through influence, not title.

Some of the biggest trust breakdowns in the industry haven't come from fraud or scandal. They came from silence.

Presence rebuilds everything. Even when strategy doesn't

What Leadership Presence Looks Like This Week

Most executives think they're being present when they send quarterly updates. Your field needs more. Real presence isn't quarterly updates. It's this:

Post 2-3 short videos casting vision. Not scripted corporate speak. Real talk about where you're going and why it matters.

Send voice memos to your top twenty leaders. Personal. Direct. "Here's what I'm thinking about..."

Show up in field Facebook groups. Comment. Respond. Be human.

Host a live Q&A addressing real concerns. No PR filter. Just honest answers to honest questions.

Share behind-the-scenes moments. Let them see you working, thinking, caring.

Invisibility is a choice, and in this profession, it's a costly one.

Zappos Was Dying in 1999

Online shoe sales seemed impossible—who buys shoes without trying them on? CEO Tony Hsieh made a bet that seemed insane: instead of competing on price, they'd compete on culture.

Every employee went through four weeks of culture training before touching a single customer. At the end, they offered new hires $2,000 to quit—ensuring only true believers stayed. Customer service calls were untimed. One agent famously stayed on a call for 10 hours and 43 minutes with a customer who just needed someone to talk to.

The result? Amazon eventually bought Zappos for $1.2 billion, not for their technology, but for their culture.

That's presence baked into behavior. Presence backed by process.

In network marketing, it's even more critical.

But yet, most corporate leaders-especially founders and executives-aren't present on the platforms where their people live.

Sure, they're on LinkedIn. But the field? They're on Facebook, Instagram, TikTok. They're watching stories. They're looking for signals.

But what they often find is… nothing.

This isn't about becoming an influencer. It's about becoming visible in the places where belief is built to last in direct selling.

Imagine if your internal comms team or PR agency helped you create just 2-3 short videos a week. Casting vision. Giving updates. Highlighting small wins.

That alone could rebuild belief faster than any promo ever will.

One legacy company in decline brought in a new executive team. Things shifted-not because of a bold strategy-but because of consistent visibility.

They showed up. Hosted raw Q&As. Owned the vision again, and the field responded.

Retention lifted. Leaders re-engaged. Belief came back-not because of incentives, but because of presence.

This profession doesn't need perfect leaders. It needs visible ones.

Leadership Isn't Strategy. It's Emotional Stability.

Especially when the waters get choppy.

When the storm hits–and it always does–everyone looks to the wheel.

Perfect captains aren't required. They need to know someone is leading.

Most field reps are directional thinkers. They interpret a dip in volume as disaster. They assume silence means collapse.

That's not logical-it's emotional, and emotion is led through presence.

Most new distributors will decide in the first twelve months whether this business becomes a hobby, a short-term stint, or a long-term path. That's why early belief-building is critical.

Stephen Covey said it best: "Leadership is communicating one's worth and potential so well that they begin to see it in themselves."

But here's what most executives miss: you can't communicate worth without communicating WHERE you're going. Good leaders have vision, but great leaders give vision. In a profession where people choose to stay every single day, casting vision isn't optional—it's survival.

That can't happen through strategy decks. It happens when someone says: 'Here's where we're going-and here's why it still matters.' But most CEOs get so wrapped up in the X's and O's of operations that they forget vision is what dots the i's and crosses the t's. Your field doesn't just want to know the quarterly plan—they want to know the legacy they're building.

Most CEOs think they're casting vision when they talk about quarterly goals. Your field doesn't care about Q3 targets. They want to know what they're building for the next decade. Here's how to connect today's actions to tomorrow's legacy:

The Vision Cascade Framework

How Great Companies Connect Today's Actions to Tomorrow's Legacy

Level 1: The 10-Year Legacy Vision Where will this company be when your current leaders retire? What will they be proud to have built?

Level 2: The 3-Year Reality Bridge What has to be true in 3 years for the 10-year vision to be possible?

Level 3: The Annual Milestones What victories this year prove we're on track?

Level 4: The Quarterly Wins What can field leaders celebrate every 90 days that connects to the bigger picture?

Level 5: The Monthly Touch Points How do you remind people monthly why their daily actions matter?

The Power: When leaders see how today's recruiting call connects to next decade's legacy, they stop just working and start building.

Who's the visible face of your company right now? Who's casting vision week in and week out? Where are they seeing you-if at all?

Because in the absence of presence, people create their own narrative. With star hunting executives constantly calling your best leaders with bigger offers, that narrative becomes: 'Maybe I should take that call.' That story rarely ends well.

Presence gets their attention. But once you have it, what keeps them? That's where most leaders fail. They think showing up is enough. It's not. You need something deeper. You need culture.

The first place trust breaks? Leadership. Because when leaders go silent, people assume the worst. In a profession where belief drives everything, the biggest leadership failure isn't executive misalignment—it's absence.

CEO Background Shapes Everything—Including Blind Spots

The direction of a direct selling company doesn't come from mission statements. It comes from the person making the calls, and most CEOs fall into predictable patterns based on where they came from.

None of these backgrounds are better or worse. But each creates blind spots that can kill companies if left unchecked.

The Field Legend Built their fortune in the trenches. Speaks fluent field. Understands the emotional drivers that make people stay or leave. They know what it feels like to get rejected, to build through doubt, to earn every rank the hard way.

Strengths: Authentic credibility with leaders. Can cast vision that resonates. Makes decisions that protect field relationships.

Blind spot: Infrastructure becomes an afterthought. They assume everyone builds like they did—with pure hustle and heart. They'll sacrifice systems for speed, thinking passion can overcome poor operations. When the company hits $50M and things start breaking, they're shocked.

The Corporate Professional Came from traditional business— pharmaceuticals, consumer goods, finance. Brilliant with forecasting, margins, and operational efficiency. They build processes that scale and systems that work.

Strengths: Creates sustainable infrastructure. Understands compliance. Makes data-driven decisions that protect the company long-term.

Blind spot: Treats distributors like employees. Doesn't understand that logic doesn't drive behavior in this profession. They'll cut events to save money, then wonder why culture died. They optimize for efficiency and accidentally destroy the human connections that drive everything.

The Founder-Visionary Never built in network marketing but sees the bigger picture. Thinks like a tech startup. Brings fresh perspective and isn't trapped by "how we've always done it." Often the most innovative companies are led by outsiders.

Strengths: Disruptive thinking. Willing to challenge industry norms. Sees opportunities others miss because they're not limited by field experience.

Blind spot: Overestimates what technology can replace. Underestimates how relationship-driven this profession really is. They'll build amazing apps that nobody uses because they solved the wrong problem.

The Hired Gun Brought in by private equity or boards to "fix" problems. Usually has a track record of turning companies around in other industries. Focused on short-term performance and exit strategies.

Strengths: Can stop bleeding fast. Makes hard decisions without emotional attachment.

Blind spot: Everything. They don't understand that quick fixes kill long-term trust. They'll cut field support to improve margins, then wonder why leaders leave. Most dangerous when they mistake motion for progress.

**Which CEO
Are You Building Around?**

CEO TYPE	VISIONARY	OPERATOR	OUTSIDER/INVESTOR
STRENGHTS	Passionate, Relatable	Efficient, Scalable	Financial logic
BLIND SPOTS	Can resist structure	Misses emotion/culture	No field credibility, Transactional

Your culture is shaped by who they are—and who you let them be.

If you're on a corporate team, this matters more than you think: you need to know which type your CEO is—and what they might be missing. If you're that CEO, self-awareness will save you years of pain.

In this profession, it's not about having all the answers; it's about seeing where your answers might be incomplete—and building the right team to fill the gaps.

Regardless of which type leads your company, one truth remains: leadership presence gets people's attention. But culture is what keeps it. And when CEOs don't understand their blind spots, they accidentally destroy the very culture they're trying to build.

Leadership presence gets people's attention. But if what you're asking them to build around isn't worth their reputation, presence becomes just performance. The foundation of sustainable belief? Your product.

If your product isn't worth talking about when no one's paying you to talk about it, you don't have a product problem—you have a business model problem.

CHAPTER 2

PRODUCTS

The field leader sits across from you in the corporate boardroom, and you can see it in their eyes before they even speak. They've been building for three years. Hit every rank. Brought in dozens of leaders. But something has shifted.

"I'm struggling to get excited about our new launch," they finally say. "And if I can't get excited, how am I supposed to get my team excited?"

That's not a motivation problem. That's a product problem.

In a profession where belief drives everything, product problems become trust problems fast.

Leadership presence gets people's attention. But if what you're asking them to build around isn't worth their time, energy, or reputation—presence won't matter. You'll watch your best leaders quietly start looking elsewhere.

Not because your comp plan got worse. Not because your culture died. But because they stopped believing in what they're actually selling.

In direct selling, your product isn't just what people buy—it's what people bet their reputation on. When leaders stop believing in what they're selling, everything else gets harder. Recruiting turns into pitching, retention becomes a grind, and your best people leave for companies where they can be proud of what they're building.

And your best people? They leave for companies where they can be proud of what they're building around.

PartyLite: When the Product Became a Commodity, the Party Ended

PartyLite collapsed not because their candles stopped burning—but because their field stopped believing.

For over thirty years, PartyLite dominated home fragrance with millions of consultants worldwide, turning living rooms into sales venues and hostesses into repeat customers. But as the world changed, PartyLite clung to nostalgia instead of doubling down on innovation, product experience, and field belief.

Here's where they missed the mark:

- **Product Excitement Died in the Field:** Candles that were once conversation starters became just another commodity you could buy cheaper at Target. Launches lost luster. Differentiation faded. The field's excitement turned to obligation.

- **No Real Product Advocacy:** The experience took center stage because the product no longer could. When your best leaders don't want to bet their reputation on what you're selling, belief disappears.

- **They Ignored the Product-First Framework:** They didn't pass the "Personal Use Test." They didn't pass the "Dinner Party Standard." And when price increases outpaced perceived value? The "Price Without Proof" sin took over.

- **Culture Became Theater, Not Genuine Engagement:** Recruiting became pitching. Retention becomes buying loyalty with incentives instead of earning it through value. And when the field starts performing instead of believing? You're already losing.

When PartyLite's direct selling model eventually struggled, the field had already lost belief. The pivot to different business models wasn't strategy—it was a response to eroded foundation.

PartyLite's products never failed them. Their belief system did. When consultants stopped genuinely loving what they were sharing and started just going through the motions, the foundation cracked.

The lesson is clear: If your product isn't the hero, your story can't last.

The Product Authenticity Crisis

Most corporate teams still don't get this: your field can smell product BS from a mile away.

They know when you're launching something because you need a Q4 bump, not because you solved a real problem. They can tell when your "revolutionary breakthrough" is just repackaging with new marketing. They feel it when you're more excited about the margin than the mission.

In an era where trust is already fragile, product authenticity isn't optional. It's survival.

Through our mastermind sessions with top earners from different organizations, the product stories are telling. Yes, the leaders who scale the fastest are often the best recruiters, but the leaders who last are the ones who genuinely love what they're sharing. They use the products. Their families use the products. They'd recommend them even without a commission check.

Because here's what happens to pure recruiters: without retention, recruiting becomes exhausting. When people don't stick, you're constantly refilling a leaky bucket. Eventually, you lose belief in what you're building. The enthusiasm fades, the recruiting slows and then stops completely.

That's the difference between building a recruiting machine and building a business built to last in direct selling.

Why Some Reps Scale and Others Stall

Same company. Same comp plan. Same product line.

So why do some people break through while others stay stuck?

It's not just hustle. It's not just who they know. It's how they think about what they're building:

Rep: Shares a product
Leader: Builds belief and transformation

Rep: Follows up to close a sale
Leader: Follows up to develop a teammate

Rep: Trades time for commission
Leader: Creates systems that duplicate without them

Rep: Talks ingredients and promos
Leader: Speaks to vision and values

Rep: Competes for attention
Leader: Creates a movement people want to join

Most reps are trying to perfect their pitch.

Real leaders shift their perspective on what they're here to do. That shift starts with how they see the product.

Corporate's Role in Shaping Product Belief (Without Babysitting the Field)

This isn't about micromanaging. But if you're in corporate, this matters:

You may not create leaders—but you shape the environment that develops them.

Here's how:

Build belief systems, not ingredient sheets. Connect products to identity, not just facts.

Reinforce transformation over transactions. Elevate testimonials, not just promos.

Create tools that challenge—not coddle. Your systems should build confidence, not codependency.

Recognize the right reps. Praise the builders, not just the closers. **Builders** focus on developing people, creating systems, and long-term growth. **Closers** focus on transactions, getting the sale, and short-term wins. Both matter, but builders create the foundation that lasts.

Give visibility to the field's rising stars. Not just the legends— highlight the ones living the product and growing real communities.

You're not the coach—but you build the arena. When that arena rewards belief, retention, and consistency—you'll get more leaders by default.

The 5 Product Sins That Kill Field Belief

Sin #1: Launching Without Living It
You've never used your own product consistently for ninety days, but you expect your field to be passionate advocates. If you're not drinking your own Kool-Aid, don't be shocked when they don't either.

Sin #2: Solving Problems That Don't Exist
You created a product because the market looked profitable, not because you identified a real pain point. When you build solutions looking for problems, the field feels it.

Sin #3: Overpromising and Under-Delivering
Your marketing promises transformation, but your product delivers incremental improvement. The gap between promise and reality doesn't just disappoint customers—it embarrasses your field.

Sin #4: Complexity Without Clarity
You built a product so sophisticated that it takes twenty minutes to explain what it does and why it matters. If your top leaders can't communicate the core benefit in sixty seconds—even for products with longer-term results—it won't duplicate.

This isn't about instant gratification. Products that deliver transformation over sixty to ninety days can absolutely work. But your field needs to be able to explain the *journey* simply: what to expect, when to expect it, and why it's worth the wait.

The test isn't "Can you show results in sixty seconds?" It's "Can you build belief in sixty seconds?" Can you help someone understand why this matters enough to stick with it? Can you paint a picture of the destination that makes the path feel worth taking?

Complexity kills duplication. Clarity creates it. Even when the results take time.

Sin #5: Price Without Proof
You're charging premium prices for commodity results. Your field becomes customer service reps defending costs instead of value evangelists sharing transformation.

When any of these sins become your reality, your product stops being an asset and starts being a liability—and in direct selling, product liability kills momentum faster than any market shift ever will.

Apple Showed Us What Product Belief Really Looks Like

January 9, 2007. Steve Jobs walks onto a stage and says five words that change everything: "Today, Apple is going to reinvent the phone."

For the next ninety minutes, Jobs doesn't talk about market share, profit margins, or sales targets. He talks about the product. How it feels. What it does. Why it matters. By the time he's done, everyone in that room—including competitors—wants one.

But here's what most people miss about that iPhone launch: Apple employees were already using prototypes. Engineers had been testing them for months. The sales team understood every feature because they'd lived with the device. When the iPhone went public, Apple wasn't just selling a product—they were sharing an experience their own people had already fallen in love with.

That's product authenticity. That's what happens when you build something so good that your own team becomes your best marketing department.

Fast-forward to today: Apple employees still get early access to new products. They don't just sell Apple—they live Apple. That authenticity translates into customer loyalty that outlasts any promotional campaign.

For direct selling, this is the standard. When your field genuinely loves what they're sharing, everything changes. Recruiting becomes referral. Objections become education. Competition becomes irrelevant.

Because you can't fake genuine enthusiasm, and you can't manufacture authentic belief.

The Product-First Framework That Actually Works

Smart companies don't just launch products—they launch experiences. They understand that in direct selling, your product is competing not just with other products, but with other opportunities. Your field is asking: "Is this worth my time, energy, and reputation?"

Here's how the best companies answer that question:

The Personal Use Test: Executive team and top field leaders use it for ninety days before launch. This builds internal belief before external announcement. Your top leaders are your reputation insurance—if they won't advocate enthusiastically, why would anyone else?

The Dinner Party Standard: Could your leaders naturally bring up your product at a dinner party without it feeling forced?

The Family Filter: Would your leaders recommend this product to family members even without commission?

The Simplicity Scale

Can a new distributor explain the core benefit in one sentence? If it takes a presentation to convey value, it won't duplicate.

Exception: High-end products with premium price points can require more explanation—but only if the complexity translates to results that justify the investment. Think luxury skincare with clinical backing or advanced nutritional systems with documented outcomes.

Even then, your field needs a simple hook: "This is the anti-aging system dermatologists use" or "This is the nutrition protocol Olympic athletes follow." The detailed explanation comes after the initial interest, not before.

The test remains: Can someone explain why this matters in one sentence? Can they create enough curiosity to earn a longer conversation?

Because if it's not simple to talk about, it won't duplicate—no matter how great the product is. Even the most sophisticated product needs a front door everyone can find.

The Results Reality Check

Are you tracking actual customer outcomes, not just customer purchases? If people aren't getting measurable results, they'll stop reordering regardless of how much they like your field leaders.

These aren't nice-to-have guidelines. They're product survival requirements in a profession built on personal relationships and personal recommendations.

The Three Product Battles You Must Win to Build a Business That Lasts

A great product or service must win all three of these battles:

Initial Purchase – Is it exciting enough to try?

Retention Worthiness – Does it make people feel different enough to stay and consistently prove its worth when money is tight?

Share-ability – Is it so good people naturally want to tell others—even without a commission?

Lose one of these battles, and everything downstream suffers.

The Four-Phase Product Filter

1 CURIOSITY SPARK
Would I even try this?

Eye-catching packaging, bold promise, or standout positioning.

2 STICKY EXPERIENCE
Do I feel something real?

First use must deliver impact—no waiting, no guessing.

3 REORDER WORTHINESS
Is it still worth my money next month?

Product holds up even under budget pressure or skepticism

4 ORGANIC SHAREABILITY
Do I naturally want to talk about it?

People share what they genuinely love—without being told to.

A product that fails at any stage leaks belief.
A product that passes all four creates momentum

Stanley: From Obsolete to Obsession

For over a century, Stanley built its reputation on rugged utility—thermoses made for blue-collar workers and outdoor diehards. But by 2019, sales had flatlined at $70 million. The Quencher tumbler had been discontinued. And the brand was quietly fading.

Enter Terence Reilly, a Crocs turnaround expert who took the reins as Stanley's global president. His insight? Stanley didn't need a new product—it needed a new story. More specifically, a new audience.

He listened. Women—especially lifestyle influencers—were begging for the Quencher's return. So Stanley partnered with The Buy Guide, a female-led influencer collective. They marketed the Quencher to teachers, moms, wellness creators—communities who didn't just want hydration. They wanted identity.

The result? Stanley's revenue exploded from $70 million in 2019 to $750 million by 2023. Same tumbler. Different message. Total reinvention.

You don't **always** need to launch new products. You need to launch new belief.

Nature's Sunshine: One Capsule at a Time

In 1972, Gene and Kristine Hughes wanted to help people take cayenne pepper without burning their throats. So they hand-filled capsules at their kitchen table in Spanish Fork, Utah.

That innovation—encapsulated herbs—launched Nature's Sunshine.

But by 1984, the company was on the brink. A poorly received compensation change created mass confusion. Earnings dropped. One-third of their field walked.

Instead of blaming the field, they owned the mistake. They reversed course, introduced medical benefits, doubled down on product education, and personally rebuilt trust.

The rebound worked. Nature's Sunshine grew to 600+ products in over forty countries. Not by hype—but by humility, innovation, and never losing sight of what mattered: trust.

Rodan + Fields: When Product Excellence Meets Network Marketing

When dermatologists Dr. Katie Rodan and Dr. Kathy Fields transitioned from retail to direct sales in 2008, skeptics were everywhere. Could premium skincare really work in network marketing? Would doctors' reputations survive the channel?

The answer was decisive: within six years, Rodan + Fields became the #1 premium skincare brand in North America, surpassing department store giants like Estée Lauder and Clinique. By 2017, they hit $1.5 billion in annual sales.

But here's what made the difference: the products were already proven. While Proactiv had generated over $1 billion in retail sales, the Rodan + Fields skincare line represented a shift—not just a continuation. They brought the credibility of the brand and clinical results, but created a premium skincare portfolio specifically for the direct selling channel.

Rodan + Fields showed what's possible when product quality meets network marketing passion. Before-and-after photos weren't marketing gimmicks—they were customer documentation. When consultants shared transformation stories, they weren't selling—they were testifying.

But their story also proves that product excellence alone isn't enough. As we'll explore throughout this book, lasting success requires the right combination of products, culture, leadership, and infrastructure. Miss any piece, and even billion-dollar momentum can unravel.

The lesson for corporate teams is clear: if you want your field to be passionate advocates, give them something worth advocating for. Not just something that pays well—something that performs well.

What Most Companies Get Wrong About Product Development

The biggest mistake isn't creating bad products—it's creating products for the wrong reasons.

Too many companies develop products backwards. They start with market opportunity, then try to engineer excitement. They launch because they need revenue, not because they identified a genuine need. They prioritize margin over mission, features over results, complexity over clarity.

But the companies that last take a different approach. They don't just listen to a few corporate executives or top distributors and call it market research. They study the intersection of multiple factors:

Culture alignment. Does this fit who we are and what we stand for?

Emerging trends. What genuine shifts are happening in the market?

Innovation opportunity. Can we solve this problem better than anyone else?

Vision coherence. Does this advance our long-term mission?

Product line synergy. Does this strengthen our existing offerings?

Smart companies start with problems their target customers genuinely experience. They create solutions that align with their culture and vision. They perfect formulations until the results speak for themselves. Only then do they think about market potential and profit margins.

That's the difference between a product launch and a product mission. Launches create temporary excitement. Missions create lasting belief; and in direct selling, belief is everything.

The AI Revolution Is Coming for Product Development

Most companies are missing the bigger AI shift: artificial intelligence is about to revolutionize how products get developed, tested, and improved. But it's also going to expose which companies are building around authentic value versus manufactured hype.

AI can analyze customer feedback in real-time, predict ingredient interactions, personalize formulations, and identify market gaps faster than any human team. The danger? Companies will be tempted to let algorithms drive product decisions instead of culture and belief.

AI can't manufacture the passion your field needs to sustain momentum. It can't create the authentic enthusiasm that turns distributors into evangelists, and it can't replace the emotional connection between a field leader and a product they genuinely love.

In the Trust Recession era, this matters more than ever. Your field can spot AI-generated hype from a mile away. They know when a product was created by committee versus conviction. They can feel when market data trumped mission.

The companies that thrive in the AI era will be the ones that use technology to create better products, not just better marketing. They'll leverage data to solve real problems, not manufacture profitable opportunities. They'll use AI to enhance the Product-First Framework—making the Personal Use Test more rigorous, the Dinner Party Standard more authentic, the Family Filter more meaningful.

Because in today's world of unprecedented AI and technology advancements, PEOPLE MATTER MORE THAN EVER! In direct selling, that human element starts with genuine product belief that no algorithm can fake.

The field doesn't need smarter products. They need products worth believing in.

AI can help you build them—but only if you remember this: **Technology serves belief. Not the other way around.**

Every product experience either builds or breaks trust.

Hope doesn't live in your welcome video.
It lives in the customer's third reorder.
And hope fades fastest when experiences don't match expectations.

People will give you grace once. Maybe twice.
But when the product doesn't back the promise, belief starts bleeding out of the business.

Hope is earned by delivering.
Retention is earned by confirming.
Culture is earned by consistently showing up.

The Real Baseline: Your Reorder Rate

Massive momentum spikes are exciting—but they're temporary.

The real question is: what happens when that energy cools?

You fall back to the baseline.
And that baseline is your **customer reorder rate**.

Track it religiously.
Know it like your revenue.
Because it's not just a metric—it's the clearest sign of whether your product is delivering real value or just riding the coattails of hype.

The best-run companies don't just chase top-line growth.
They build for sustainability by **obsessing over reorder behavior**.

Because that's what lasts.

The Reality Check: Will Your Product Make the Cut?

During economic downturns—or even just personal budget crunches—every customer becomes an evaluator.

They keep the essentials: housing, groceries, insurance.
Then they look at what's left—and they start cutting.

So here's the only question that matters:

Did your product make the cut?

If it didn't?
You never had a customer.
You had a transaction.

Too many companies assume once the sale is made, the job is done. Wrong. The sale is the *start* of belief.

That's why ongoing product marketing matters:

- Facebook groups for customers

- Drip campaigns that educate without spamming

- Retention rituals that resell the experience again and again

The moment a customer invests, they want to be reminded why it matters. They don't resent the marketing. They crave the belief.

Services Matter Just as Much—But Work Differently

Everything we've said about products applies to traditional network marketing services too—travel, energy, wellness, credit protection, and digital education.

(This doesn't include licensed professions like real estate, insurance, or financial planning, which follow different regulatory rules and business models.)

If you're selling these services, you're not off the hook.

Would people stay without compensation? Are you delivering results they can feel? Is the experience seamless, supported, and sticky?

A great service should:

- Solve a real pain point

- Inspire a story

- Build community through shared use

If you're selling access, not value, your retention will expose you.

Don't Fear Amazon—Out Serve It

Your biggest threat probably isn't the FTC. It's Amazon.

You're not going to win by being slightly cleaner, or slightly more affordable, or slightly faster to ship.

You win by offering what Amazon can't:

A culture that builds belief

A community that supports transformation

An education system that develops loyalty

A field that amplifies results through relationships

Where there's challenge, there's also opportunity. Amazon forces us to level up. It forces better pricing, better storytelling, better retention, better systems.

That's not a threat. That's a gift. If you build for it.

Community as Product

Your customer didn't just buy a capsule, a shake, or a subscription.

They bought into something.

Something that should make them feel better. Something that should help them become better. Something that should connect them with others doing the same.

Too many companies separate product from culture. But they're connected.

Build a Facebook group. Launch a drip campaign. Create 21-day challenges. Do something that reinforces belief post-purchase.

Your customers need to be resold—not manipulated, but re-engaged. Every month. Every reorder. Every new product.

Because when hard times hit, people don't cancel what they believe in—they cancel what they tolerate.

Make sure you're not just tolerable. Make sure you're vital.

The Safety Net for Your Leaders

Here's what no one wants to say out loud:

If you build only around leaders, you'll eventually feel held hostage by them.

This is not a knock on leadership. Leaders matter. They must be respected, recognized, and resourced.

But the best way to protect your company—and your leaders—is to build a customer base so solid that no individual departure causes a collapse.

That's the gift of product belief. It creates stability. It reduces drama. It builds something you can depend on.

Not just at the top—but all the way down.

The Product Retention Connection

Your product is a critical piece of your retention strategy—but it's not the only piece.

As we'll explore throughout this book, retention requires the right combination of leadership presence, culture, recognition, development systems, and infrastructure. But here's what most companies miss: if the product foundation is weak, none of those other elements can compensate.

Customers don't stay because of your compensation plan—they stay because your product works. Distributors don't build long-term because of fast-start bonuses—they build because they're proud of what they're sharing.

When someone gets real results from your product, they become retention-proof. They're not just a customer—they're a case study. They're not just using your product—they're proving your product.

But when products fail to deliver, everything becomes harder. Customer acquisition costs go up. Retention rates go down. Your field starts managing objections instead of sharing results. Eventually, your best people leave for companies where they can be proud of what they're building around.

You can have world-class culture, perfect compensation, and amazing recognition systems. But if your product doesn't deliver, retention will always be an uphill battle.

The 90-Day Product Reality Check

Every quarter, corporate teams should ask these five questions:

1. **Are we personally using our own products consistently?** If leadership isn't living the product experience, how can they expect the field to?

2. **Are customer reorder rates improving or declining?** Reorder rates don't lie—they're the ultimate measure of product satisfaction.

3. **What are customers saying in private, not in public?** Survey data and testimonials tell one story. Social media comments and support tickets tell another.

4. **Can our leaders describe the key outcome clearly enough for a 10-second conversation?** If explanation requires education, you've got a duplication problem.

5. **Would we still stand behind this product if we had zero financial interest in it?** This isn't about compliance—it's about authenticity.

Remember: successful companies just do the basics better.

These questions aren't meant to create paranoia. They're meant to create clarity. Because clarity about your product reality is what lets you build everything else with confidence.

Product Excellence as Competitive Advantage

In an industry where compensation plans get copied, marketing messages get mimicked, and top leaders get recruited away, product excellence is your only sustainable competitive advantage.

No patent protects passion. No trademark guarantees transformation. And no recruiter can save a bad product.

But when you've got something that genuinely works—something your field is genuinely excited to share—everything else becomes easier. Recruiting becomes referral. Retention becomes natural. Culture builds itself around shared success stories.

That's not marketing speak. That's business reality in a profession where personal recommendation drives everything.

The companies that survive the next decade won't be the ones with the flashiest launches or the most aggressive compensation plans. They'll be the ones whose field leaders genuinely love what they're sharing.

Because you can't fake authentic enthusiasm, and in direct selling, authentic enthusiasm is what separates movements from moments.

Bottom Line

Your product isn't just what people buy—it's what people bet their reputation on. If your field isn't excited to share your product when no one's watching—and no one's paying—they won't build around it. But when belief is real, results are visible, and culture multiplies that belief—you don't need to push. They lead. And others follow. That's how you build something that lasts.

Your product isn't just what people buy. It's what people bet their reputation on. If your field isn't excited to share your product when no one's watching—and no one's paying—they won't build around it. But when belief is real, results are visible, and culture multiplies that belief—you don't need to push. They lead. And others follow. That's how you build something that lasts.

Culture isn't what you say.
It's what you do and what people
feel when no one's watching.

CHAPTER 3

CULTURE

What people feel most is whether they're growing or just going through the motions. Culture without personal development becomes stagnant. People sense when an environment is helping them become better versus just helping them earn more. The companies with the strongest cultures understand this: transformation creates loyalty that transactions never will.

The team meeting felt different. You couldn't put your finger on it, but the energy was off. The usual enthusiasm was replaced by polite nods. People checked their phones more. The jokes that used to get laughs fell flat. Your top builders sat quietly in the back instead of up front. Something had shifted in the culture, and you were the last to notice.

Six months later, you'd learn that three of your best leaders had been quietly building elsewhere while still showing up to your events.

That's not a recruitment problem. That's a culture problem.

Leadership presence gets people's attention, but culture is what keeps it.

Culture isn't your slogan, it isn't your convention theme and it's definitely not what you slap on a PowerPoint slide—It's what people feel when no one's watching.

What 1,700+ Top Earners Are Really Saying About Culture

Through our mastermind sessions with top earners from different organizations, a pattern emerges consistently. Companies confuse culture with events—thinking bigger conventions equal stronger culture, louder recognition equals deeper connection, more company swag equals more loyalty. But culture isn't what you do, it's what people feel.

What I've learned from hosting masterminds with top earners across different companies is that culture problems show up the same way everywhere: in the gap between what companies say and what they actually reward.

The most common culture killers I hear about: celebrating only the top 1% while the middle 80% feel invisible, talking about "family" during good times but cutting people the moment numbers drop, preaching values in meetings but making decisions that contradict everything they claimed to believe.

One theme that keeps surfacing: star hunting executives who protect toxic top earners because they're afraid to lose the volume. These leaders destroy team culture while executives look the other way, more concerned about poaching the next big name than developing their own people. I've learned about organizations where the CEO went silent during tough times, leaving the field to wonder if anyone was steering the ship. There are companies that think culture means having the best swag or fanciest events while their daily operations make people feel like numbers instead of humans.

The pattern is always the same: when there's a gap between what you say and what you do, culture dies. In a profession fighting to rebuild trust, broken culture isn't just a problem—it's toxic.

When Howard Schultz Walked Back Into Starbucks in January 2008, He Found a Company in Crisis

The crisis was deeper than anyone imagined. Same-store sales had dropped 8% in fiscal 2008—the worst performance in company history. Stock price had collapsed from $40 to under $8. Wall Street analysts were calling for immediate store closures and mass layoffs to stop the hemorrhaging. Customer complaints were flooding in about watered-down coffee and assembly-line service. The iconic espresso machines that built the brand had been replaced with push-button automatics so tall that customers couldn't see baristas' faces. The hand-ground coffee aroma that made Starbucks feel like home? Gone—masked by breakfast sandwiches that made every store smell like a fast-food joint.

This wasn't just poor performance. This was a company watching its soul dissolve in real-time while 200,000 employees wondered if they'd have jobs next month. Schultz had stepped down as CEO eight years earlier, and his successors had prioritized growth over culture, efficiency over experience. Now the bill had come due, and it was devastating.

Schultz made the most expensive decision in company history: on February 26, 2008, he shut down every single U.S. store for three hours. 7,100 locations. Complete shutdown. $6 million in lost revenue in one afternoon—just to retrain 135,000 baristas on what coffee was supposed to taste like. Critics called it a publicity stunt. Wall Street called it financial suicide. But Schultz spent the next eight months working shifts in stores across America, talking to customers, listening to what had broken. He discovered the push-button machines were alienating customers who wanted to see their drinks being crafted. He found that standardized menus didn't work in different neighborhoods. He brought back the coffee aroma, literally redesigning ventilation systems to let the smell escape into the streets.

Within eighteen months, same-store sales rebounded 19%. Stock price doubled, then tripled. Employee satisfaction scores hit all-time highs. Customer loyalty returned with a vengeance. Starbucks didn't just survive—they transformed into the global powerhouse that exists today, with over 35,000 stores worldwide and a market cap exceeding $100 billion. Schultz proved that when you fix the culture, you don't just fix the numbers—you fix the future.

Wells Fargo Proved That Fake Culture Destroys Everything Faster Than Any Competitor Ever Could

For 150 years, Wells Fargo was America's most trusted bank—the place you'd trust with your grandmother's life savings and your kid's college fund. They built their reputation on two words: unshakeable integrity. Then in 2009, everything changed. New CEO John Stumpf brought Wall Street pressure that would destroy 150 years of trust in just seven years. Corporate set impossible sales targets—eight products per customer, regardless of need. Branch managers who missed quotas faced public humiliation and termination. Employees were told to "jump on the stagecoach or find another job."

What happened next was predictable and devastating. Desperate employees did what desperate people do: they faked it. Between 2009 and 2016, Wells Fargo employees opened 3.5 million fake accounts, enrolled customers in credit cards they never requested, and charged fees for products that didn't exist. Customers discovered phantom accounts when reviewing statements. Some were charged overdraft fees on accounts they never opened. Others saw their credit scores damaged by cards they never applied for.

The scandal exploded in September 2016. CEO John Stumpf resigned under pressure, forfeiting $41 million in compensation. The fallout was swift and brutal: $185 million in initial fines that eventually grew to $3 billion. 5,300 employees fired, including senior executives. Stock price dropped 24% in two months. Customers closed over 1.6 million accounts. The brand that took 150 years to build was destroyed in 18 months.

But here's what's remarkable: the board finally woke up. They fired Stumpf, overhauled the bonus system, and tied executive pay to actual customer satisfaction instead of sales quotas. They refunded $142 million to wronged customers and set up a whistleblower hotline that employees actually trusted. It took five years and billions in fines, but trust slowly started to return. Sales targets became customer-focused. Employee surveys showed renewed confidence. The company learned the hardest lesson in business: culture isn't what you say—it's what you reward.

Network Marketing Runs on Different Rules

In this profession, culture isn't optional. It's oxygen, and it matters more here than almost any other business model—because this is a volunteer army.

Your leaders don't have to show up. Your customers don't have to stay. Your field doesn't owe you anything.

You can't pay people to care. That's culture.

What I've observed from leaders who build lasting cultures across different companies: they share three common approaches.

They celebrate behavior, not just outcomes. They make people feel seen at every level, not just the top. And they align their systems with their stated values—no mixed messages.

It shows up in everything:

- How leadership presence drives belief (Chapter 1)

- How you develop leaders instead of buying them (Chapter 6)

- How retention is engineered, not hoped for (Chapter 8)

- How events create transformation, not just information (Chapter 9)

- How people are recognized, seen, and valued (Chapter 5)"

Network marketing isn't a job. But it runs on human behavior, and human behavior responds to feeling seen, valued, and believed in.

The Tension Every Direct Sales Company Faces

FIELD CULTURE	CORPORATE CONTROL
Relationship-first	Systems and scale
Messy, emotional, human	Policies and protection
Built on belief, not just comp	Built on predictability

Built to Last companies respect both—but lead with culture.

Corporate teams often want to create culture—but they don't build in the field. They don't run the systems. They're not the ones closing customers or onboarding new recruits daily.

Culture can't be forced. But it can be reinforced, protected, and elevated.

The biggest blind spot? Successful CEOs think they can manage a volunteer army like employees. They focus on systems and metrics while their culture quietly hemorrhages the leaders they can't afford to lose. They're overconfident in their traditional company success and think they know what drives performance. They've run companies where people show up because they have to. They assume the same management principles apply to a volunteer army.

They focus on systems, metrics, and operational efficiency—all important things. But they miss the fundamental difference: in direct selling, people choose to be here every single day. Culture isn't nice-to-have. It's the only thing that keeps people from walking away.

What keeps me sharp is hearing from leaders across different companies in our mastermind sessions—seeing how culture plays out differently even when companies use similar language.

Some companies say "we're family" and actually treat people like family. Others say "we're family" and then cut people the moment numbers drop. Some companies say "we value integrity" and make decisions that protect long-term trust. Others say "we value integrity" but excuse bad behavior when it comes from high producers.

The difference isn't the words. It's the follow-through.

But how do you know if your culture is strong or quietly cracking? Most companies find out too late—when their best leaders are already planning their exit. Here's how to diagnose your culture before the damage becomes irreversible:

▶ THE CULTURE AUDIT: WHAT GETS MEASURED GETS MANAGED

Most network marketing companies treat culture as an afterthought. They think if they just recruit enough people, the rest will sort itself out.

That's like trying to fill a bucket with water while ignoring the holes in the bottom.

Recruiting more people (pouring in water) doesn't matter if your culture (the bucket) is cracked and leaking. You need both: momentum and infrastructure. Culture is infrastructure.

Peter Drucker said it best: "What gets measured gets managed." So let's measure your culture.

The Culture Cancer Test

Rate each statement on a 1-10 scale (1 = completely false, 10 = completely true):

1. **Leaders feel safe giving honest feedback**. No fear of retaliation or being labeled "negative".

2. Recognition is consistent, meaningful, and not just reserved for top ranks. Everyone has a path to being seen.

3. **Communication between corporate and field is clear, two-way, and regular**. Not just corporate talking at the field.

4. **There is alignment between stated values and actual decisions.** You walk the talk when it counts.

5. **Field leaders understand the company's vision and feel included in it**. They're building toward something, not just building.

6. **Corporate actively listens and adjusts based on field feedback**. Input leads to actual changes.

7. **Mid-level leaders feel empowered, not overlooked**. The middle isn't forgotten

8. **The company is consistent**—no constant directional changes. Stability over shiny object syndrome.

9. **There is trust in corporate's competence and intentions**. The field believes you know what you're doing.

10. **Leaders believe this company is built to last, not just chasing the next wave**. Legacy mindset over quick wins.

HOW TO USE THIS SCORECARD

Step 1: Internal Assessment
Each senior corporate leader completes this individually. No group discussion until after scoring. Average your corporate team's responses.

Step 2: Field Reality Check
Send the same scorecard to 30-50 field leaders across different levels:

- Top 5% earners (your stars)

- Mid-tier builders (your backbone)

- New leaders under 6 months (your future)

- Former leaders who left in the last 12 months (your mirror)

Step 3: Face the Truth
Compare corporate vs. field averages. A 2-point gap is concerning. A 3+ point gap is a red flag that demands immediate attention.

Step 4: Close the Gaps
Pick your three lowest-scoring areas. Build a 30-60-90 day action plan. Assign ownership. Set deadlines. Measure progress.

Companies that ignore these gaps watch their best leaders get recruited away by competitors who make them feel valued. The companies that face recognition gaps head-on build cultures where leaders turn down bigger offers to stay.

What Actually Works: For Corporate Teams

Check what you're actually rewarding.
I've seen companies celebrate the wrong things for years, then wonder why their culture feels fake. Are you reinforcing values—or just volume? If you only celebrate rank, don't be shocked when people chase vanity metrics over real behavior.

Talk to 5 new reps this month.
Ask: "What was your first impression?" and "What felt confusing or disconnected?" Then shut up and listen. Don't fix it mid-call. You'll learn more in those conversations than from any survey.

Fix the first 72 hours.
The first few days set the tone for everything. Make it personal. Make it simple. Make it build confidence, not confusion.

Celebrate behavior, not just results.
Every month, spotlight someone for being consistent. Helpful.
Coachable. Loyal. Show your field what you actually value.

Let them see your values in action.
The field imitates what they see. Let them see you valuing people—not
just performers.

The strongest cultures aren't built by corporate alone or field alone—they're
co-created. When corporate tries to control culture from a boardroom, the
field feels excluded. When the field creates culture without corporate input,
it lacks consistency. The magic happens in the collaboration.

Supporting the Field (Without Controlling It)

Build with leaders, not for them.
Form councils. Create collaboration groups. Let top leaders shape the
initiatives instead of just receiving them.

Give tools, not rules.
Share frameworks and resources—but let the field own delivery. They
know their people better than you do.

Support their grassroots efforts.
Encourage launch pods, local meetups, private accountability chats—
even if they're messy. Show that you see them building.

Protect culture from poison.
One toxic top earner can destroy what ten builders are creating. Don't
let volume excuse bad behavior.

Make sure your comp plan matches your culture.
If your plan rewards chaos, don't expect calm. If it rewards sprints,
don't expect sustainability. Design matters.

Culture is the person behind the paycheck.

It creates belonging. Loyalty. Growth that's built to last in direct selling.

It connects all the chapters in this book.

If people only feel it when the music's on, you don't have culture—you have your performance.

Companies that don't align culture with systems in the next twelve months risk losing up to 40% of their field leadership to competitors who do.

But here's where most companies make their biggest mistake: they build strong culture, then destroy it with compensation plans that reward exactly the opposite behavior. If your comp plan is your biggest selling point, it will also be your biggest liability.

Leadership presence gets people's attention. But culture is what keeps it.

Culture isn't what you say. It's what you do and what people feel when no one's watching.

If your comp plan is your biggest selling point, it will also be your biggest liability.

CHAPTER 4

COMPENSATION

The CFO slides the spreadsheet across your desk at 4:47 PM on a Friday. "If we keep paying out at this rate," she says quietly, "we'll be insolvent in eighteen months." You stare at the numbers. Your 'industry-leading' comp plan—the one you've been bragging about for three years—just became your death sentence.

The irony stings: the very thing that built your momentum is about to destroy your company.

But here's what's really dangerous: most comp plans start out fine. The problem isn't the original design—it's what happens when growth stalls and panic sets in.

That's when the deals start.

The performance agreements that pay significantly above normal comp rates, depending on the leader's track record.

The "bridge bonuses" that guarantee minimum monthly income while leaders "build their foundation." The rank advancements that let recruited leaders skip qualification periods everyone else has to earn through. The override deals that unlock deeper commission levels immediately instead of over time.

You tell yourself it's "performance-based recruiting." The contracts have quotas. There are benchmarks to hit. It's merit-based—the bigger the leader, the better the deal.

But your field sees it differently. They watch a recruited leader making 200% of what they earn for the same volume while someone else gets 130%—and they're getting base rate. They see newcomers accessing commission levels that took them years to unlock, and they start asking dangerous questions: "Do I really need to walk away just to be valued?"

The performance tiers make you feel strategic about the deals. But the field mathematics don't lie—you're now running multiple compensation plans: premium rates for recruited elite, standard rates for homegrown leaders, and everyone knows it.

You can build the strongest culture in the industry. But if your compensation philosophy undermines it, you'll watch your best leaders walk away.

The field doesn't just want to get paid. They want to believe what they're building is sustainable.

Stop Telling Your Field You Have "The Best Comp Plan in the Industry"

It instantly kills credibility.

Best? Based on what? Have you studied all the comp plans out there? There are thousands. Of course not.

Even if you had, it changes nothing because the field doesn't care about theoretical best.

They care about three things:

- Can I win?

- Can others win?

- Does this plan make sense?

What they don't want is smoke, and that's what most companies offer when they lead with hype.

MonaVie Proved This Inside Our Profession

In the late 2000s, MonaVie was the darling of network marketing. They reached nearly $1B in sales faster than almost any company before them. Their product was simple. Their branding was elite. Their events were legendary.

But their compensation strategy? It was built to spike-not sustain.

To drive momentum, MonaVie gave distributors upfront contracts-sometimes with no strings attached. Big money to join. Fast checks for early builders. Recognition became elite-driven. Most of the volume was fueled by hype-not deep customer loyalty, and it worked for a while.

But as growth surged, so did expenses. Their payout model left little room for innovation, events, or operational stability. So when the hype wore off, so did the belief.

The same leaders who ran fast left even faster. Customer retention tanked. Cash flow dried up, and the company was eventually absorbed.

It's not that MonaVie didn't have vision. Or talent. Or systems. It's that they mistook hype for health-and momentum for loyalty.

They tried to buy growth instead of earning it.

The beauty of cross-pollinating ideas between successful leaders is seeing what compensation strategies actually create longevity.

Leaders who've built sustainably share three common insights: They focus on behavior-based rewards, not just outcome-based payouts. They design plans that reward staying, not just starting, and they understand that complexity kills duplication.

Some people now refer to them as the billion-dollar bust. Not because they didn't achieve massive success-but because the foundation wasn't built to last.

To be clear, this isn't a jab at the incredible leaders and people inside that company. I personally had friends in MonaVie who built the right way-with integrity, strategy, and belief.

But systemically, the company rewarded flash over fundamentals. They built a short-term recruiting machine instead of a long-term retention model.

That's why MonaVie became a case study on what not to do for the entire profession. It's why deal-making today comes with skepticism.

Because when private equity vultures over-leverage companies with debt and hype, pay people just to show up, and outsource culture to contracts—it always cracks. They're more interested in quarterly extraction than long-term construction. In an era where trust is already fragile, compensation disasters don't just hurt companies— they damage the entire profession.

What you build it with is how it stands-or falls.

When growth stalls, panic kicks in. Companies try to protect margin— cutting comp plans, lowering product quality, or scaling back support. But each cut chips away at belief. And once belief starts decaying, trust soon follows. This creates the doom loop: cuts to protect margin destroy the very belief that drives future growth.

Netflix Found a Different Way

September 2001. Netflix is hemorrhaging money and about to die. The dot-com crash wiped out their funding, Blockbuster is launching a competing service, and Reed Hastings just laid off one-third of his workforce—120 people in a single day. The remaining employees are terrified they're next. Hastings realizes that traditional management is killing what's left of the company. So he makes a radical decision: he eliminates the vacation policy, throws out performance reviews, and tells people to 'act in Netflix's best interest.' The keeper test becomes brutal but honest: if you wouldn't fight to keep someone, let them go immediately. The best people get autonomy.

The result? Streaming is born. Netflix pivots from mailing DVDs to inventing binge-watching. They go from under a million subscribers to over 260 million by 2024. The company's culture deck becomes Silicon Valley gospel. Top talent stays, and the company moves faster than anyone else.

Netflix never promised the highest payouts. They aligned compensation with results-rewarding performance, retention, and innovation.

That's why they scaled globally while others stalled.

Through our mastermind sessions where top earners openly discuss compensation realities, you realize most plans reward the wrong things.

Network marketing has dozens of comp plans that look good in a PDF-but melt under real-world momentum.

Too many companies reward recruiting, overpay on fast starts, and then pray people stick. They don't balance margin. They don't design for scale. They design to look good on paper.

Then volume drops, and panic kicks in. Your top leaders start fielding offers. You're forced to cut commissions or burn cash. Either way, you lose the people you built the company around.

If someone comes in because of a deal—they'll leave because of a deal quick-fix executives who chase quick recruitment fixes instead of building sustainable systems are just feeding the revolving door that's weakening our profession's core structure.

The Compensation Death Spiral: How Panic Kills Companies

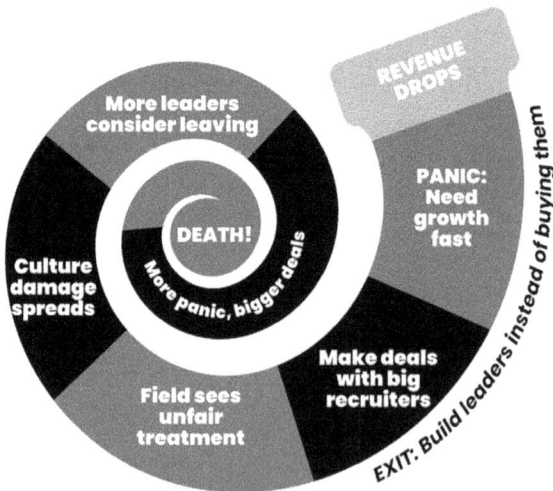

If someone joins because of a deal, they'll leave because of a deal.

It's not just about paying too much. It's about what kind of culture you create.

If your culture is built on hype and incentives, not loyalty and belief-you're not building on rock. You're building on sand.

That was the heart of MonaVie's collapse.

The most stable network marketing companies understand something simple: A comp plan isn't just about payouts. It's a philosophy.

A great plan:

- Rewards the right behavior

- Protects the company's ability to grow

- Creates belief at every level

- Makes people feel like they're winning

Most people won't hit the top ranks. But the smartest companies are finding ways to incentivize meaningful action at all levels.

That's why we're seeing more activity-based incentives.

Instead of basing a trip purely on rank, companies are adding front-end qualification metrics that anyone can earn-like sponsoring X customers or Y team members over a 60-day window.

Even better? They're offering partial qualifications. Earn the flight. Pay for the hotel. Or earn hotel nights and cover your own airfare.

Either way-people feel like they won, and when people feel like they've won, they stay engaged.

Trips aren't just a luxury. They're a culture builder. They give corporate a chance to influence, to connect, to unify. They help people see a future that's bigger than just a comp plan payout.

This is what great compensation strategy looks like built to last in direct selling.

It's not "how much can we pay?" It's "how do we build loyalty, reward production, and keep people playing the long game?"

▶ THE COMPENSATION COLLAPSE PREDICTOR

Most companies won't overhaul their comp plan — and they shouldn't. The bigger the legacy, the bigger the risk. But that doesn't mean they should fly blind.

This Comp Plan Health Check gives corporate teams a tactical, measurable way to assess their plan's health across three essential pillars:

1. Sustainability

2. Behavior Alignment

3. Retention & Progression

You don't need to reinvent the comp plan. But you do need to know if it's working.

FRAMEWORK: COMP PLAN HEALTH CHECK

For each question below, rate yourself on a scale of 1–10. Then average your totals by section. Use feedback from corporate execs, top field leaders, and a sample of new reps to score each section for better accuracy.

SECTION 1: SUSTAINABILITY (Average these 1–10)

- What % of field commissions are tied to actual product sales, not recruiting?

- What is your breakage rate (unpaid/retained bonus pool)?

- Is your comp plan payout sustainable for long-term operations? (Consider your specific product margins)

- Are most top earners paid from the volume they generate, or via overrides from deep levels?

- Have your commission ratios stayed stable over the last 12–24 months?

- Do your rank advancement bonuses pay out on real volume, or just recruitment spikes?

SECTION 2: BEHAVIOR ALIGNMENT (Average these 1–10)

- Are new reps earning $300–500/month within their first 60–90 days at a measurable rate?

- What % of new reps make their money back in the first 30–60 days?

- What % of your total payout goes to reps who have sponsored at least one new customer or builder in the last 30 days?

- Does your plan reward repeat order behavior over front-loaded volume?

- Do your bonus structures incentivize retention and reactivation, or just new acquisition?

- Are you allocating separate reward pools (trips, spot bonuses, promo money) to reinforce desired behaviors without messing up the core comp plan?

SECTION 3: RETENTION & PROGRESSION (Average these 1–10)

- What % of your ranked leaders are still at that rank 90 days later?

- What % of rank achievers go on to hit the next rank within 180 days?

- Do you track the average time it takes reps to hit their first rank?

- Are there "dead zone" ranks where most reps stall out? If so, do you know why?

- Do your incentives and bonuses support long-term leadership development or just quick hits?

- Have you mapped how your comp plan contributes to monthly field attrition vs. growth?

SCORE INTERPRETATION:

- 8–10 average per section: Healthy and strategic. Keep optimizing.

- 5–7 average per section: Caution. You're likely bleeding talent or misaligning incentives.

- Below 5: Urgent. Fix it before the field sees what you can't.

Avoid Becoming the Old Navy of Network Marketing

Smart compensation isn't just about the plan itself—it's about how you support it. One of the fastest ways to train your field to devalue your compensation is through promotion addiction.

Companies think they're being smart with constant promotions.

You see it all the time in retail. Ask anyone in North America when the last time was that they paid full price at Old Navy. They'll laugh. Because no one does.

Why? Because everything is always "on sale." The sale is no longer the exception. It's the expectation.

That might work for T-shirts. It doesn't work for network marketing.

In this profession, promotion overload creates a false high. It inflates checks, drains inventory, and trains the team to chase short-term wins over long-term strategy. Distributors get a dopamine spike one month and a crash the next. You're manufacturing momentum—and that momentum comes with a hangover.

Worse, it rewires the field. New builders don't know how to grow unless there's a promo. Leaders stop focusing on fundamentals. Customers become discount addicts, and eventually, it backfires.

Now you're running promotions just to get back to baseline.

Promotions aren't bad. But they need guardrails.

Here's what smart companies do:

- Create a promo calendar (public or private) with strategic spacing
- Rotate product categories so teams don't get stuck on just one item

- Tie promotions to activity-based challenges not just discount codes

- Watch inventory so that leaders don't overload and stall reorders for 3 months

- Analyze promo ROI beyond just the initial spike—look at 60-day reorder data and field retention

Remember, if the goal is to build real businesses, promos should amplify momentum—not replace it.

Constant promotions train people to never pay full price.
Ask anyone about Old Navy. Everything is always 'on sale,' so nothing feels valuable.

OPTIONAL COLLABORATION IDEAS:

- Work with top field leaders to co-develop promo bonuses that drive right behavior.

- Use corporate surveys or rep focus groups to learn why certain ranks are sticky and others are dead zones.

- Offer 3-month rank audits to top earners: "What do your team's comp behaviors tell you?"

Great compensation creates belief, not hype.

When that's in place, the field doesn't need to compare you to anyone else. They'll feel it. They'll believe it. And they'll stay.

No homegrown leaders + field full of mercenaries = expensive revolving door.

How you pay people is your culture. Period.

Smart compensation gets people in the game. But recognition keeps them playing. And here's what most companies miss: what you celebrate doesn't just reflect your culture—it becomes your culture.

You can build the strongest culture in the industry. But if your compensation philosophy undermines it, you'll watch your best leaders walk away.

If your comp plan is your biggest selling point, it will also be your biggest liability.

*If you only recognize the top
1%, don't be shocked when the
99% stop showing up. What you
celebrate becomes your culture.*

CHAPTER 5

RECOGNITION

The team leader who built your fastest-growing leg just posted her resignation on Facebook. Not to you. Not to corporate. To Facebook. "After three years of building," she wrote, "I finally realized I was just a number to them. Time to find a company that actually sees me." Sixty-seven comments of support. Zero from your company.

That's not a compensation problem. That's a recognition problem.

Smart compensation gets people in the game, but recognition keeps them playing. And here's what most companies miss: what you celebrate doesn't just reflect your culture—it becomes your culture.

Recognition isn't just about applause. It's about shaping behavior.

The 10 vs 10,000 Problem

In fact, if you only recognize the same ten people on stage, you've already lost the other 10,000.

This is the invisible majority crisis plaguing our profession. Companies spend thousands flying in the same top earners to tell the same success stories while their backbone builders—the ones actually doing the daily work—watch from the shadows.

The field mirrors what you celebrate.

If you want more builders, recognize the builders. If you want more customer growth, spotlight the customer gatherers. If you want culture? Highlight the quiet, consistent reps showing up every week.

Recognition isn't just for the top. It's not just about ranks, cars, or checks.

Jeunesse Showed What Happens When Recognition Tips Wrong

Jeunesse hit a billion dollars in revenue faster than nearly any other network marketing company at the time-explosive momentum, huge international growth, and leaders hitting high ranks at a rapid pace.

Their Diamond rank became the symbol of success-touted as averaging over a million dollars a year. But as the company scaled, recognition became laser-focused on those ranks. From the outside, it felt like only the elite mattered and the everyday builder? Forgotten.

At events, it became top-heavy. Spotlights were reserved for the inner circle. The field could feel it. New reps didn't see a path for themselves, and that's where belief started leaking out.

When recognition becomes an exclusive club instead of an inclusive culture, it weakens the foundation. This is exactly what private equity vultures want—a culture so focused on the top 1% that the middle 80% become disposable, making it easier to cut costs and extract profits.

This wasn't just a Jeunesse problem. It's a common mistake when companies grow fast and lose sight of what bought their momentum in the first place-everyday wins from everyday people.

Salesforce Proved What Happens When Recognition Becomes the Engine

Dreamforce started in 2003 with 1,000 people crammed into a San Francisco hotel ballroom. Marc Benioff had a crazy idea: what if a software conference felt more like a rock concert? By 2019, Dreamforce had exploded to 170,000 attendees, generated $150 million in local economic impact, and commanded a global livestream audience of millions. But here's what most people miss: Dreamforce isn't just an event—it's Salesforce's retention engine. Customers who attend Dreamforce have reported retention rates as high as 92%, significantly higher than those who don't attend. The three-day experience generates more customer loyalty than millions in advertising ever could. Customers become evangelists. Retention hits 92%. New products launch live, and every attendee leaves feeling like they built the company. Dreamforce isn't an event. It's the engine that keeps Salesforce's community glued together. The energy is contagious— people come back year after year, not for the swag, but for the feeling that they're part of something bigger. Meanwhile, most network marketing companies treat events like afterthoughts. Meanwhile, too many network marketing companies treat events like afterthoughts. Dreamforce costs millions because they know the ROI of belief.

That's what recognition does when it's built right. It creates belonging.

Now take that truth into network marketing.

When done right, recognition creates loyalty. When done wrong-or not at all-it creates silence. And silence kills belief.

Five Levels of Recognition That Actually Matter

Private Recognition

Sometimes a personal message goes further than a public one. Handwritten notes. Direct messages. A quick voice memo from the exec team. Small gesture. Big impact.

Peer-to-Peer Recognition

Create systems where the field recognizes each other. Team shoutouts. Culture awards. Monthly "unsung hero" spots. Let the team own the spotlight.

Milestone Recognition

Not just ranks. Celebrate things like: first customer, first paycheck, first launch event, 90-day streaks, team service and contribution.

Stage Time That Reflects Reality

Don't just give the mic to the top 1%. Give the mic to the ones with the habits you want others to duplicate.

Leadership Visibility Recognition

When execs go out of their way to highlight new leaders, it sends a signal: We see you. You matter. We're watching the right stuff.

Recognition That Builds Culture (Not Just Hype)

Recognition systems that work understand a crucial difference: celebrating results vs. celebrating the activities that create results.

But there's an even deeper layer: recognition that celebrates personal growth—not just performance—creates the culture that retains people long-term. When you spotlight someone's journey from timid to confident, from inconsistent to disciplined, from follower to leader, you're not just recognizing them. You're showing everyone else what's possible. That's the recognition that makes people want to stay and grow, not just show up and perform.

Most companies recognize results. The problem? Results are always delayed.

Recognition that only celebrates rank advancements or top salespeople creates two toxic effects:

1. 95% of the field gets ignored

2. Leaders only get rewarded when they finish—not when they fight

Smart companies don't try to recognize every activity from corporate. That's impossible at scale. Instead, they build systems that empower field leaders to recognize the right activities.

The best companies create recognition frameworks their leaders can use:

- Activity tracking templates leaders can customize

- Weekly recognition toolkits with suggested categories

- Simple dashboards that show team activity (not just results)

- Recognition training for field leaders on what activities to celebrate

- Corporate spotlights that highlight field leaders who recognize activity well

Corporate's job isn't to recognize every follow-up call. It's to train field leaders why activity recognition matters—then give them tools to do it.

Because when a brand new person shows up to a team Zoom and hears recognition for someone who sent ten invites—not just the top recruiter—they start thinking: "I can do that too."

That's the beginning of duplication, and duplication is the beginning of momentum.

When you build systems that help field leaders recognize activity, you're not just celebrating what happened—you're programming what happens next.

What Works: Corporate Moves That Build Culture

Audit your event recognition system.
Who's getting on stage? Why? Does it reflect the behavior you want more of-or just the status you think earns applause?

Give the field better tools.
Recognition templates, weekly shoutout ideas, and coaching on what to look for beyond rank. Most team leaders want to recognize people-they just don't know how.

Break down your leaderboards.
A single ranking isn't enough. Create categories: new rankers, customer gatherers, consistent performers, comeback stories. Let more people win.

Celebrate progress, not just perfection.
The journey gets love, not just the destination. The mom who hit her first $300 check in six months of part-time effort? That story is more relatable than a million-dollar earner.

Make stories real, not just impressive.
Feature people your field can actually see themselves in becoming.

Recognition isn't fluff. It's fuel. The desire to feel important drives more behavior than money ever will. This insight comes up consistently when top earners share what really motivates their teams.

▶ BUILDING A RECOGNITION ENGINE (NOT JUST MOMENTS)

Field Recognition Systems That Scale:

Dedicated Recognition Coordinator. Someone whose job is spotlighting field reps: birthdays, rank ups, achievements big and small.

Public social shoutouts. From regional managers and GMs. Let them go on personal timelines, not just business pages. This feels personal.

Micro-content strategy
15-second video clips recognizing someone's quote or moment. Corporate can batch this weekly.

Executive touch points
Quick texts or voice notes from leadership at key milestones—first 3 customers, first rank advancement, etc.

Thoughtful gifts at milestones
Flowers for first team rank. Leadership books for coaching new rankers. Personalized plaques for anniversaries.

Handwritten cards
Not for every rank. But used selectively, they're unforgettable.

Recognition hierarchy
Smaller ranks celebrated regionally. Mid-tier company-wide. Top-tier at events and global communications.

Duplicate the system
Make recognition templates available to field leaders so they can model the same behaviors in their teams.

You are what you recognize.

You can say retention matters. But if you only celebrate enrollments—retention doesn't matter.
You can say you care about the part-time builder. But if they never feel seen—they'll assume they don't belong.

Recognition proves your values louder than any mission statement ever will.
When people feel important, they stay. When they feel invisible, they scroll away.

Smart companies are starting to leverage AI to track consistency, spotlight unsung heroes, and personalize recognition at scale.

Recognition doesn't have to be manual—it just has to feel meaningful.
AI gives you the ability to automate with heart. Recognition tied to daily disciplines—not just outcomes—compounds belief.
It reinforces the Slight Edge: simple actions repeated over time become unstoppable momentum.

AI is going to revolutionize how we do this. Recognition can now be tracked, triggered, and delivered automatically.
But just because it's automated doesn't mean it has to feel robotic.
The best companies will use AI to make recognition more personal and timely.
Imagine a leader getting a custom shoutout sixty seconds after hitting a milestone. That's the future.

Don't misunderstand me—I strongly believe in AI's potential. But it will only deliver results for leaders who understand how to leverage it properly. That distinction will become a critical competitive advantage

Most companies focus on the transaction—the sale, the rank, the bonus. But retention happens beyond the transaction. It's in the unexpected support, the behind-the-scenes recognition, the moments that make people feel seen.

Recognition drives repetition.
And what gets repeated becomes your culture.

In a profession working to rebuild credibility, what you celebrate either builds trust—or destroys it.

Don't build a moment. Build a system.
One that makes people feel seen early and often—especially when they're still becoming who they want to be.

But here's where most companies make a critical mistake:
They think recognition alone creates leaders.

It doesn't.

Recognition without development just creates dependent performers who need constant validation.
Your top earners aren't automatically your best leaders.

Hard truth:
Stop chasing stars. Start raising workhorses.

Smart compensation gets people in the game.
But recognition keeps them playing.

And here's what most companies miss:
What you celebrate doesn't just reflect your culture—it becomes your culture.

The Risk of Spreadsheet Leadership
 Some companies are trying to spreadsheet their way to legacy.
 But you can't optimize your comp plan, automate your onboarding, and surgically cut your culture—then act surprised when belief erodes.

Gordon Hester put it perfectly:
"Hope is nothing more than our belief systems about the future, and it is created from the experiences we have with people."

Our profession doesn't run on perfect decisions. It runs on belief.
And when leaders stop listening—when field experiences don't match the vision being cast—belief evaporates.
Trust isn't built in metrics.
It's built in moments.

Stop chasing stars.

Start raising workhorses.

CHAPTER 6

LEADERSHIP DEVELOPMENT

Strong systems create growth. Strong leaders create momentum. But strong cultures create legacy.

Let's get this straight. There is no long-term business without leadership development. You can throw all the money in the world at incentives, ads, funnels, and compensation tweaks—but if you're not developing leaders, you're just building a customer base with an expiration date.

In direct selling leadership is your real product, everything else is packaging.

Every field leader talks about wanting more leaders. Here's what's crazy: most aren't developing leaders. They're just watching people recruit and hoping someone rises.

Leadership development isn't hope. It's not chance. It's structure, feedback, and progressive challenges. It's one of the most duplicated missing systems across direct selling.

Somewhere along the way, our profession got lazy. Instead of developing leaders, we started chasing them. Instead of growing farms, we started chasing stars. You know exactly what I'm talking about. Leaders constantly being poached. Corporate executives on the phone throwing bonus agreements. Entire companies structured around who can swing the next big fish from someone else's downline.

Same revolving door. Same desperate playbook.

Through speaking in twenty three countries and hosting elite masterminds for top earners, the superstar hunting stories are identical across every company. The same leaders getting the same calls. The same promises. The same contracts—though today's deals almost always include performance clauses, clawbacks, or rank requirements. The era of blank checks is over.

Leaders get the organization they deserve.

If someone joins because of a deal, they'll leave because of a deal. If you build your foundation on hype and contracts, don't be surprised when it sinks.

You don't build legacy on star power. You build it on systems that raise up consistent, coachable, workhorses who buy in early and grow through the ranks.

Dexter Yager Proved What Happens When You Build Leaders Instead of Buying Them

In 1964, a beer salesman from upstate New York joined a five-year-old company called Amway. Dexter Yager had no business background, no network, and no shortcuts. What he had was a simple philosophy: "This business only works if you truly love people and want to help them succeed."

By the time Yager passed away in 2019, he'd built the largest network marketing organization in history. Over one million distributors across forty countries. $2.6 billion in annual sales at peak. His organization became one of Amway's largest and most influential networks. But here's what made Yager legendary: he didn't buy a single top leader from a competitor. Instead, he created them.

Yager didn't just mentor leaders—he built systems that manufactured them. While other companies were chasing big names, Yager was perfecting the art of duplication. He pioneered the motivational tape system that became the backbone of network marketing training. Every week, distributors received cassette tapes with actionable training they'd listen to during commutes, then discuss with their teams. The brilliance wasn't the content—it was the consistency. Leaders across 40 countries were getting the same message, the same mindset, the same methodology.

His small-group "dream sessions" became legendary. Yager would sit with eight to ten emerging leaders, help them map out five-year goals, then create accountability systems to track progress. Bill Britt started as a struggling distributor who almost quit. Through Yager's personal mentorship, Britt built his own million-distributor organization. Tim Foley went from factory worker to industry icon using the same leadership development pipeline.

But Yager's genius was in the multiplication. Every leader he developed was immediately taught to identify and mentor their own "next generation." This created leadership depth at every level, not just at the top. New distributors weren't just learning to sell products—they were learning to develop people.

The culture Yager built rewarded patience, not performance theater. Recognition at Yager Group events wasn't just about sales volume.

Leaders were celebrated for developing other leaders, for consistency over time, for building sustainable teams. Annual conventions attracted thousands, with workshops on everything from mindset to advanced leadership. The message was clear: this is a marathon, not a sprint.

The retention rates proved it worked. While other organizations churned through distributors, Yager's teams had leaders who stayed for decades. His own children rose through the ranks based on performance, not bloodline. The system created loyalty because it created genuine opportunity for anyone willing to learn and grow.

Compare that to what happened at Jeunesse. Dexter raised thousands of leaders who could stand on their own. Jeunesse stacked stars at the top without duplication underneath—and it collapsed when the stars left. Influence isn't enough. Influence without infrastructure is a time bomb.

While Yager was building systems that lasted decades, modern companies chose the opposite path.

Google Proved That Teams Beat Geniuses Every Time

Early Google was obsessed with hiring the smartest people on paper— Stanford PhDs, MIT engineers, candidates who could solve impossible brainteasers in interviews. For years, they believed raw intelligence was everything. Then Project Aristotle flipped the script. After studying 180 teams over two years, Google discovered something shocking: their highest-performing teams weren't filled with geniuses. They were filled with people who felt safe to speak up, admit mistakes, and challenge ideas without fear. Their best teams weren't built on lone geniuses. They were built on trust, psychological safety, and collaboration. Google ditches the brainteasers, focuses on team fit, and sees innovation spike. Google Docs, Gmail, Maps—none of those came from lone wolves. They came from teams that trusted each other. Internal data showed that employees who felt safe to speak up were twice as likely to stay and three times as likely to be rated top performers.

Build teams that last. When you develop leaders from within instead of constantly recruiting from outside, you create something sustainable.

The Leadership Ascension Framework

There's a reason most companies are stuck in a cycle of retraining, rehiring, and rebuilding. They treat leadership as a title, not a journey. The highest performing organizations in direct sales don't just have good leaders—they have systems that create leaders.

Real leadership evolves in stages:

Lead Self. Personal accountability, consistency, mindset. Show up. Execute your daily actions. Hit your baseline goals. Stop asking for credit before results.

Lead Followers. Basic influence, team support, duplication. Plug people into the system. Teach the basics. Run your own onboarding and team calls.

Lead Leaders. Vision casting, systems building, multiplication. Coach others to duplicate. Launch initiatives. Build a sustainable recruiting pipeline. Cast vision.

This framework is how you diagnose leadership gaps at every level of your organization. And it's how you reverse the burnout curve by giving people clarity on how to grow without grinding.

The Leadership Development Flywheel

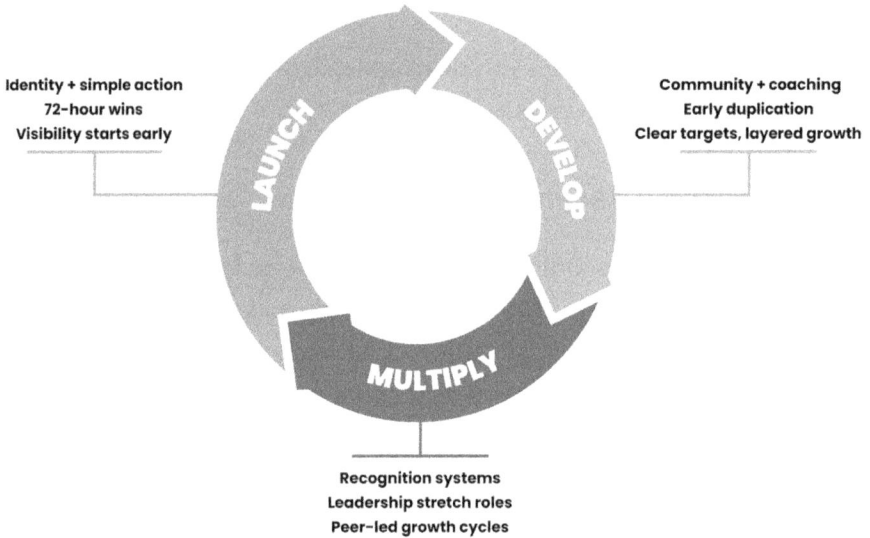

Identity + simple action
72-hour wins
Visibility starts early

Community + coaching
Early duplication
Clear targets, layered growth

LAUNCH

DEVELOP

MULTIPLY

Recognition systems
Leadership stretch roles
Peer-led growth cycles

Then tie access to opportunity. Want the advanced training? Earn it. Want to co-host the next team event? Hit the benchmarks. Want access to monthly leadership calls? Lead five team presentations and two accountability groups.

Create pathways. Reward behavior. Build belief that's built to last in direct selling.

Direction Over Information: The 72-Hour Leadership Test

Duplication is not a speech. It's a system. Building leaders isn't about information dumps. It's about giving clear direction that anyone can follow. Most companies kill duplication in the first 72 hours by overwhelming new people with product encyclopedias, compensation plan deep-dives, and company history lessons. Then they wonder why nothing sticks.

The best onboarding happens in the first 72 hours. That's where belief is built—or broken. Most companies drown new people in PDFs, logins, and product info. But new people don't need information. They need direction.

You've got a 72-hour window to set identity, pace, and simplicity.

Here's what works:

- 3 immediate action steps (no more)

- A simple script for first reach outs

- Clear expectations for visibility and support

- One rank target + one timeline

If your first three days are focused on orientation instead of activation, you're not duplicating leaders. You're duplicating indecision.

The leaders who develop other leaders understand something simple: you can't duplicate what you can't remember. Here's what works: give new team members 3-5 simple action steps for Day 1. Think: "Send this message to three people, watch this 5-minute video, schedule your launch call for this weekend." No backstories. No overwhelming choices.

The most duplicatable phrase in this profession? "I just got started, and I'm excited. Can I get your opinion on something?" New people can say that with confidence because it's true. Veterans can't.

Direction beats information every time. Your goal isn't to make them experts—it's to make them active. Because active people stay. Confused people quit.

Companies that master this create leaders who can onboard others the same way. Companies that don't create leaders who feel like they need a PhD before they can invite their neighbor.

The Leadership Factory Blueprint

Every direct selling company should ask: Are we a leadership factory or a sales machine?

Here's the difference:

SALES MACHINE vs LEADERSHIP FACTORY

SALES MACHINE	LEADERSHIP FACTORY
Focused on monthly volume	Focused on long-term leadership
Rewards production only	Rewards development and promotion
Reacts to cycles	Builds for stability
Overtrains new people	Equips future leaders, not just sellers

You don't scale by managing more people. You scale by multiplying more leaders.

As mentioned earlier in this chapter, it's easier to cut a check than it is to build a system. It's easier to recruit a name than it is to develop a leader. But if you're serious about building something that lasts, your entire culture needs to shift from acquisition to ascension.

This dual framework splits leadership development into two lanes: what corporate can measure and what the field can execute.

Corporate-Facing: Duplication Diagnostics

Don't guess. Use real indicators. Here are the metrics corporate teams can actually track to measure leadership development effectiveness:

Key Performance Indicators:

- % of recruits who place a second order within 30 days. Proxy for successful onboarding and engagement

- % of active reps with at least one personally enrolled active rep in the last 90 days. Indicates duplication vs. stalling

- Ratio of customers to reps per leader. Shows if they're building customer volume or just recruiting

- % of rank advancements maintained for 90+ days. Separates real growth from volume spikes

- Volume concentration per leg. Reveals how deep and balanced the structure is

- Leadership rank to total revenue ratio. Tracks if the leadership pool is growing or shrinking

Critical Warning: If your comp plan rewards short-term spikes but you aren't tracking how long those ranks are held, you're measuring the wrong thing.

Field-Facing: Suggested Field Growth Blueprint

This is non-intrusive guidance. Corporate isn't micromanaging. They're equipping. Structure this as a suggested checklist that corporate can provide to top field leaders and let them run with:

Sample Checklist for Field Leaders:

- Are you running 72-hour action plans for new recruits?

- Do your leaders understand and track taprooting?

- Are DMO/WMO systems documented and modeled by top earners?

- Do new builders get a launch script or coaching call within their first week?

- Are leadership committees or growth pods in place for mid-rank mentorship?

- Do your teams have weekly IPA (income-producing activity) scoreboards?

Framing Note: Top field leaders are already doing these things. But corporate can provide the structure, recognition, and backend tools to make adoption easier—without telling the field how to lead.

Implementation Approach

Corporate Role:

- Track the duplication diagnostics monthly

- Provide tools and recognition for field leaders hitting growth benchmarks

- Create systems that support field-driven initiatives

- Fund leadership development without controlling methodology

Field Role:

- Own the execution of leadership development

- Adapt corporate tools to their team's specific needs

- Drive accountability and mentorship at the grassroots level

- Share best practices across teams organically

Integration Principle: Field duplication is the lifeblood of direct selling. Corporate doesn't own the how—but they do influence the when, where, and what gets reinforced. Smart companies build quietly behind the scenes and let leaders take the spotlight.

What Corporate Can Actually Do

Collaborate with top leaders to co-create leadership pathways instead of dictating them. Use rank milestones to trigger access to development resources, not just bigger checks. Host leadership intensives at corporate for mid-rank leaders who are showing up consistently. Bring in third-party experts to train on systems, mindset, and execution—remove the politics. Fund the system without controlling the field. Support leadership development without hijacking it.

Everyone's Chasing the Big Break

Everyone's chasing the big break. The overnight win. But the compound effect doesn't work like that. It's the slight edge. The micro-decisions. The five minute follow-ups and consistent action. Not sexy, but it stacks. Most people want quantum leaps. What they need is quiet repetition; that's the real flex.

Organizations that continue star hunting instead of developing leaders will find themselves with no bench strength when market conditions shift. This profession is under attack by private equity vultures who see our companies as quick profit extraction opportunities. We don't need more star hunters feeding their greed. We need better farmers building something they can't touch.

Raise workhorses. Develop depth. And watch what happens.

What This Looks Like This Week

- Diagnose your team: Who's Leading Self, Leading Followers, Leading Leaders?

- Audit your 72-hour onboarding: Is it information overload or action-focused?

- Stop chasing stars: Identify three workhorses you can develop this month

The fastest way to lose momentum is to keep training the same people for the same role over and over.

Final Thought: Responsibility Before Rank

The best cultures promote people before the comp plan does. You want to see who's ready? Give them responsibility before recognition. If they rise, build around them. If they flinch, that's feedback.

Leadership development isn't glamorous. It's repeatable, and that's what makes it powerful.

You can develop all the leaders you want and create the strongest leadership development culture in the industry. But if you can't keep the people you're growing, you're just training talent for your competitors. Because leadership development gives you the people. But personal development gives you the foundation. Without both, you're teaching leaders to build on sand.

Leadership development creates the structure. Personal development creates the staying power. You don't build a business. You build people, then people build the business. That's the truth Zig Ziglar understood decades ago, and it's more relevant today than ever.

CHAPTER 7

PERSONAL DEVELOPMENT. YOU DON'T BUILD A BUSINESS. YOU BUILD PEOPLE, THEN PEOPLE BUILD THE BUSINESS

Personal growth precedes business growth. Without people development, business won't reach its potential. Without retention through personal development, you're just cycling through people instead of developing them.

People join for many reasons, money, products, opportunity, but they stay because they feel seen.

Let's stop pretending this is just about commissions and compensation plans. Leadership development without personal development is like building a house without a foundation. You might get the structure up, but it won't last. The truth? Personal development is the person behind the paycheck.

You can have the best products. The flashiest promos. The smoothest onboarding. But if people aren't growing, they're eventually going. Period. People don't stick around because they earned $282 last month. They stay because they're becoming someone they're proud of. That's the real win.

They came to make money. They stayed to become more.

This Profession Was Built on Growth—Before Instagram Made It a Hashtag

This profession was built on personal growth before Instagram made it a hashtag. Back when Dexter Yager was handing out tapes. When Mary Kay Ash was training people on gratitude journals before personal branding existed.

Somewhere along the way, personal development became an accessory—something cute you sprinkle on after you close the sale. But without it, people don't stick. Without it, your team starts looking like a sales floor, not a community.

Personal development is what keeps people from quitting after the first "no." It's what helps someone bounce back after their family ghosts them in group texts for pitching the product. This isn't fluff. It's the difference between building leaders and recycling casualties.

If you remove personal development from the equation, what's left? Just a compensation plan and a box of product. That's not a movement. That's a transaction.

Mary Kay Got This 60 Years Ago

Mary Kay Ash built her empire on a simple philosophy: "We teach people and then teach products." Her sales force didn't just sell cosmetics—they attended weekly meetings focused on goal-setting, confidence-building, and leadership skills. The pink Cadillacs weren't just recognition; they were symbols of transformation.

Mary Kay Ash didn't build an empire by teaching lipstick. She built it by teaching values. She wrote personal thank-you cards to every leader. She called consultants personally to congratulate them. She created a culture of belief before bonuses. That's why Mary Kay still exists today—60+ years later—with a global footprint.

Her consultants would say, "I came for the lipstick, but I stayed for the person I became." That's personal development. That's what most companies today are still missing.

The Four Types of Growth—Only One Creates Loyalty

I've spent the last two decades leading, training, and watching thousands of top earners up close, and the ones who last? It's not because they made six figures fast. It's because this profession *changed* them.

They're better spouses. Better parents. Better humans.

I'm one of them.
I'm a better father, husband, neighbor, friend, and leader because of what I've learned here.
You can't put that in a comp plan—but it's the reason I'll never leave.

Growth happens in four ways inside this profession:

- **Knowledge** – Books, podcasts, trainings. Fuel for the mind.

- **Skills** – Scripts, objections, communication. Fuel for confidence.

- **Character** – Resilience, humility, consistency. Fuel for trust.

- **Vision** – Belief in something bigger. Fuel for long-term action.

But there's a fifth kind of growth that matters most: identity.

That doesn't mean everyone becomes a leader.
Some just want to stay close to the fire. They love the community, the purpose, the feeling of progress.
But when people find a version of *themselves* they like more… they stay.

Not because they have to.
Because they want to.

It's the quiet shift from "I do network marketing" to "This is a part of who I am."
That's what creates staying power.

The Truth About Burnout

Burnout doesn't start with exhaustion.
It starts with disconnection.

Disconnection from belief.
Disconnection from identity.
Disconnection from purpose.

Nobody burns out just from working hard.
They burn out from carrying **high hopes** with **low clarity**.
They burn out from **over giving** in relationships where they feel invisible.
They burn out from **tying their worth** to a business that exposes every insecurity. And they burn out when the mission that once lit them up… now feels heavy, uncertain, or lonely.

This business isn't just about selling products or recruiting people.
It's about putting your heart on the line.
It's about dreaming in public—and risking rejection from the people who know you best.

That emotional risk doesn't just create pressure.
It creates fragility. Because when someone's self-worth is fused with their business performance, every "no" feels like a personal verdict.

Burnout is more than being tired. It's being **tired of being tired**. It's when the gap between your expectations and your reality grows so wide, you stop believing the work is worth it.

That's why personal development isn't optional. It's the oxygen mask. It's the fuel.
It's what gives people the resilience to keep going—not because it gets easier, but because *they* get stronger.

The High-Stakes Emotional Reality

When you're dealing with a business built on extremely high hopes that can help you achieve your dreams, when you connect money with your deepest aspirations, you're also dealing with all of your fears. And then on top of that, you're dealing with human beings and relationships and you're dealing with the mother of all fears—the fear of judgment.

This business asks people to dream big. To invite their family. To post on social media. To believe in something that others might not understand. That's not just professional risk—that's personal exposure. When someone puts their reputation on the line for their future, the stakes feel life-changing.

The fear of judgment runs deeper than most people realize. It's not just "What if they say no?" It's "What if they think I'm desperate? What if I fail publicly? What if I'm not cut out for this?" Those fears don't disappear with a better script or a new app. They disappear with personal development.

The 3 Types of Burnout in Direct Sales

Nobody sticks around if they don't learn how to lead a Zoom, manage their energy, and actually finish something they start.

The reps who last?
They don't just develop skills.
They develop **perspective**.

Because burnout doesn't always come from doing too much; it comes from believing it's **all pointless**.

And that belief shift—the one that turns chaos into clarity—*that's* what personal development is for.

Here's how I break it down:

Emotional Burnout
Caused by rejection, isolation, and fear of judgment.
They're drowning in content but starving for direction.
They don't need another PDF, they need perspective.

Identity Burnout
Caused by trying to "be someone" instead of becoming yourself.
They joined to change their life… but they don't recognize who they're becoming.
They're stuck in comparison instead of growth.
Only perspective realigns them.

Action Burnout
Caused by spinning their wheels on unproductive activity with no results.
They're pouring into everyone else—but no one's pouring into them.
They feel invisible in their own business.
Perspective reminds them of *why* they started.

And underneath all of it?
That root system of fear:
Fear of judgment.
Fear of failure.
Fear of being exposed.

That's why personal development isn't fluff.
It's what keeps your head above water when momentum slows.
It doesn't just help you grow.
It helps you **see things clearly again**—and that's what prevents burnout before it starts.

Personal Development Is the Fuel, Not the Fix

Running a business without personal development is like owning a car with no gas. It can be the nicest car in the world. But if the tank is empty, you're not going anywhere.

Think of personal development like a car. You're the driver. The system is the vehicle. Your compensation plan, your products, your team—that's the car. But personal development? That's the gas.

You still need to turn the key, put it in drive, and steer. You still need to put your foot on the pedal and navigate the road. Personal development doesn't drive for you. But without gas in the tank, it doesn't matter how hard you press the pedal or how good your steering is. You're not going anywhere.

Personal development doesn't drive the business for you—but it gives you the fuel to show up, steer, accelerate, and keep going when things get hard.

Here's what I've learned working with thousands of different people: oftentimes your voice falls on deaf ears. They need that constant outside voice—books they're reading, podcasts they're listening to, stories that resonate. That outside voice matters. When your own belief is shaky, it's those books, audios, mentors, and community that speak life into you.

Because eventually, it sinks in. And when it does, they don't just believe in the company, they believe in themselves.

Motivation Without Motion Is Useless

Motivational quotes don't build momentum. Motivation without motion is just noise. You can read thirty seven books and still be stuck. The best cultures don't just inspire. They create movement. They get people out of their head and into simple action.

Personal development without application is just entertainment. The goal isn't to make people feel good for an hour. It's to give them tools they can use when things get hard. When their warm market stops responding. When their new recruit doesn't show up. When they're staring at a rejection and wondering if they should quit.

PD vs. Procrastination Development

Let's call out the elephant in the room:
Not all personal development is real development.
Some of it's just procrastination in disguise.

In *Your Rank Advancement Blueprint*—my book on all levels of leadership—I call this the **LaLa Principle.**
Learn. Action. Learn. Action.
That's how it's *supposed* to work.
But too many turn it into:
Learn. Learn. Learn. Learn. Learn… maybe act once.

They confuse being busy with being productive.

They binge podcasts.
Buy every course.
Take notes.
Feel inspired.
And do nothing.

Motivation without motion.
Self-help with zero execution.

And companies?
They're just as guilty.
They bring in speakers. Drop quotes. Run rah-rah calls that feel good for a moment…
Then nothing.

No assignments.
No habits.
No tracking.
No follow-through.

And then they wonder why the field doesn't change.

Most people don't need more books.
They need to do *something* with the ones they already read.

Why Personal Development Multiplies Duplication

Want better leaders? Help them grow personally. Because you can't teach what you haven't lived. A confident leader teaches confidence. A disciplined leader inspires discipline. A grateful leader models gratitude.

Personal development builds leadership bench depth. And that multiplies faster than any script ever will. In a volunteer army, people need reasons beyond money to stay engaged. Personal development provides those reasons. It creates connection, progress, and purpose that outlast any comp plan adjustment or market dip.

What Smart Companies Build In

Here's what it looks like when companies get it right:

Weekly calls or zooms include mindset segments. Not just strategy—real personal growth content. Ten minutes on how to lead yourself. Five minutes on how to stay consistent. Not fluffy nonsense—real, tactical growth they can use in life and business.

Recognition celebrates character, not just checks. Highlight someone's confidence, consistency, or courage. "She used to be afraid to speak. Now she's leading team trainings." That hits harder than any volume bonus. We are always sharing the TRANSFORMATION.

Events feel like growth conferences, not just business updates. People leave inspired about their potential, not just informed about systems. The most powerful part of any event isn't the script—it's the way people walk out seeing themselves differently.

Reading becomes part of the culture. Teams that read together, grow together. Book-of-the-month clubs. Development challenges. Recognition for finishing personal growth books. Low cost. High impact.

Personal Development That Actually Sticks

Here's how you create a PD system that drives retention:

Make it visible – Recognize readers, learners, and sharers weekly.
Make it relevant – Tie growth content to business results.
Make it social – Create PD challenges or share threads.
Make it measurable – "What did you implement this week?"
Make it repetitive – Create a list your recommended books.
Make it safe – Create space for vulnerability and growth.

The Business Case for Personal Development

Want to increase retention? Invest in belief. Want higher average order value? Teach confidence. Want consistent recruiting? Develop identity.

You can keep tweaking your comp plan—or you can invest in the culture that keeps people showing up when their paycheck is small and their dreams still feel far away.

The AI Factor: Why Personal Growth Is Now Job Security

Let's be blunt.

AI can already write your emails, automate your customer follow-ups, and close a decent percentage of your orders.

If all you're offering is *more information or a faster script*—you're replaceable.

But the one thing AI can't replace?

Who you're becoming.

Empathy. Grit. Trust.
The ability to lead humans, not just manage tasks.
That's what keeps people in this profession valuable.

That's what personal development creates.

We're not in the information age anymore.
We're in the *application* age.

Side hustles are no longer optional.
Reputation is currency.
Confidence is the skill set.

If your people aren't growing emotionally, mentally, and socially…
They're getting outrun by someone who is.

Personal development isn't a perk—It's survival.
For the field.
For the leaders.
For the companies who want to stay in business five years from now.

The Retention Math of Personal Development

Here's what most companies miss:

Yes, that $200–500 a month matters.
It pays for groceries. Gas. Guilt-free Target runs.
It gives people permission to keep going.

But what actually keeps them?

Who they're becoming in the process.

Remove that growth element—and the check starts to feel transactional.
Replace it with belief, confidence, and purpose—and now it's emotional income too.

When companies cut the development piece, they think they're saving time. What they're really doing is shortening their shelf life.

Because when someone likes who they're becoming, they stay longer, contribute more, and stop shopping for a new company.

Transformation always beats transaction.

This Is the Invisible Glue Holding Your Field Together

People already pay to be part of transformation. They tithe to churches. They hire therapists. They buy mastermind access. They chase growth. Why? Because deep down, everyone wants to become a better version of themselves.

This business—when done right—gives them that. It's not just a paycheck. It's a growth journey wrapped inside a business model.

No one sticks with a business that only grows their wallet and not their world.

Bottom Line

Hype doesn't duplicate. Short-term motivation doesn't scale. Legacy isn't built on quick wins.

But you can build something that lasts when you make personal development part of the culture—not the add-on. The strongest organizations combine leadership development systems with personal growth culture. They know that technique without transformation creates performers, not leaders. And sustainable growth requires both.

Because in a volunteer army, the only thing stronger than a product is a purpose. And personal development is what makes that purpose real.

Leadership development gives you the people. But retention gives you the foundation. Without both, you're building on sand.

CHAPTER 8

RETENTION

If you're not obsessed with retention, you're not in business. You're just spinning the wheel—celebrating promotions while ignoring the silent exits.

This chapter is about how to fix that.

Retention isn't a "support function." It is the business.

You can hire the best influencers. Launch the flashiest product. Cut the biggest checks. But if you don't keep customers, it all collapses.

"If you're bleeding out customers, nothing else matters. Retention is the scoreboard. Everything else is just noise you use to feel better.

Too many companies focus on the wrong retention. They roll out a new system, hype it for two weeks, and then vanish. It's fire-and-forget thinking—and it kills trust. The best programs aren't flashy, they're consistent. They worry about keeping top earners happy with bigger bonuses while their customer base quietly disappears.

Customer retention drives everything else. No customers, no commissions. No commissions, no field retention. No field, no business.

Retention Is Built, Not Bought

COMP PLAN

STRATEGIC RECOGNITION

SIMPLE ACTION WINS

LEADERSHIP VISIBILITY

COMMUNITY & CULTURE

PERSONAL DEVELOPMENT IDENTITY

**Belief doesn't come from one layer.
It's the compound effect of everything working together.**

When you're curious about patterns across companies, you start asking different questions. Instead of 'What's our retention rate?' the question becomes 'What's different about customers who stay versus those who leave?' Instead of 'How do we reduce churn?' it's 'How do we accelerate lifetime value?'

A lot of corporate teams still think of retention as something the field handles. That mindset? It's outdated—and it's costing you millions.

In the best companies, customer retention is owned at the corporate level—from the first click to the fourth reorder.

Costco proved what happens when you treat people right.

Costco pays $17 an hour. 88% get health insurance. Wall Street calls it "waste." CEO Jim Sinegal spends weekends on the floor, knows people by name, keeps snacks in the break room. Turnover? 6%. Industry average? 60%. Customer renewal rate? 91%. Costco's stock beats Walmart and Amazon.

The principle works for employees and customers: treat them well, give them value, and they stick around.

For direct selling, retention is the whole game at every level. Keep your corporate team. Keep your field leaders. Keep your customers. All three feed each other.

The data shows customers who make it past four months are exponentially more likely to stay long term.

Not kind of likely. Not sort of likely. Like, lifetime-value-multiplier likely.

So your job as a company is to build a system that gets them to month four. Then optimize from there.

This isn't one campaign or one dashboard. This is your operating philosophy.

Quick-fix executives are terrible at customer retention. They get a new customer, deliver a product, then go silent while planning their next flashy launch. These executives mistake acquisition campaigns for retention strategy. Most quick-fix executives outside PE aren't villains—they just haven't been in the channel or studied the business long enough. Hence, read this book.

No post-purchase journey. No nurture path. No feedback loop. Just a countdown to cancellation.

Companies spend 90% of their effort hunting new customers and 10% keeping the ones they have. Then they act shocked when people cancel. Then they blame the field for "poor customer service." It's not the field's fault, it's yours.

Corporate owns customer retention. The field can support it. But it's your responsibility to engineer it.

Every hour that goes by without action from a new customer decreases your odds of keeping them.

You should treat the first 48 hours like urgent care. What happens in those hours sets the tone.

Your distributor's #1 job is to bring in new people. Your job is to keep those customers.

Whatever the field does for customer retention is a bonus. But you are the insurance plan.

If someone buys and never hears from the company again, that's your fault. If they don't know where to go next, that's your fault. If they cancel and no one ever asks why? Also your fault.

Customer retention needs to be engineered. Not hoped for.

Cross-Company Retention Patterns

Through our mastermind sessions with top earners from different organizations, a pattern emerges consistently. The beauty of cross-pollinating ideas between successful leaders is seeing what translates universally.

Leaders who consistently maintain high customer retention share three common approaches: They treat the first purchase as the beginning of education, not the end of the sales process. They create micro-wins in the first thirty days that build confidence. They connect customers to community, not just product.

What I've learned from hosting masterminds with top earners across different companies is that retention problems show up the same way everywhere: in the gap between what companies say and what they actually reward.

Some companies say they value retention but only celebrate new acquisitions. Others talk about customer focus but design their entire recognition system around recruiting metrics. The pattern is always the same: when there's a gap between what you say and what you do, retention dies.

After hearing the same challenge from leaders in different organizations, you realize retention isn't just a number on a dashboard, it's a lived experience that varies dramatically company to company. Some companies create customers who become raving fans. Others create customers who quietly disappear. The difference isn't the product, it's the experience after the purchase.

THE LEAKY BUCKET DIAGNOSTIC

Retention is the quiet crisis. If you don't track it, you'll blame the wrong thing when the field stalls. And if your culture is leaking people faster than you're enrolling them, no product launch or comp tweak will save you.

As we discussed in Chapter 3 regarding compensation plans, you can't growth-hack your way out of a retention crisis. Just like comp plans that reward flash over fundamentals eventually collapse, retention problems compound until they destroy momentum.

This scorecard helps corporate teams diagnose retention weaknesses, spot warning signs, and benchmark performance in real-world terms. Rate each area on a 1-10 scale, then compare scores across three perspectives: corporate leadership, top field earners, and new participants.

Section 1: Customer Retention Metrics

Rate your performance on a 1-10 scale:

Retention Timeline Performance:

- **3-Month Customer Retention Rate.** What % of customers are still ordering after 90 days?

- **6-Month Customer Retention Rate.** What % maintain activity through the critical 6-month mark?

- **12-Month Customer Retention Rate.** What % become long-term, loyal customers?

Customer Behavior Indicators:

- **Average Order Frequency**. How often do active customers reorder per month?

- **Time to Churn Analysis**. Do you track the average days from enrollment to drop-off?

- **Return/Refund Trends.** Are refund requests increasing, stable, or decreasing?

- **Customer-to-Rep Conversion**. What % of customers eventually become distributors?

Section 2: Field Retention Metrics

Rate your performance on a 1-10 scale:

Field Retention Timeline:

- **90-Day Rep Retention**. What % of new reps are still active after their first quarter?

- **6-Month Rep Retention**. What % survive the critical 6-month learning curve?

- **12-Month Rep Retention**. What % build sustainable, long-term businesses?

Field Performance Indicators:

- **Incentive Achievement Rate.** What % of reps hit at least one bonus, incentive, or rank advancement?

- **High Earner Ratio.** What's the ratio of top 10% earners to total active field?

- **Activity Consistency.** Average number of weeks with zero commission activity per rep?

- **Rank Retention**. What % of rank advancements are maintained for 90+ days?

Section 3: Internal Red Flags

Rate your systems and culture on a 1-10 scale:

Leadership Awareness:

- **Field Intelligence**. Do your field leaders know and discuss customer retention statistics?

- **Recognition Alignment**. Are leaders celebrated for long-term retention or just volume spikes? (This connects back to our discussion on recognition in Chapter 4)

- **Incentive Design**. Are rewards/trips built for velocity or consistency?

System Integration:

- **Segmentation Strategy**. Do you send different nurture sequences to reps vs. customers?

- **Tracking Infrastructure**. Do you monitor how long reps stay before going inactive?

- **Feedback Loops**. Are retention insights shared with product development and marketing teams?

Three-Perspective Scoring Framework

Complete this assessment from three viewpoints (similar to our Culture Audit approach in Chapter 2):

Corporate Self-Assessment: Each C-level executive and VP scores independently, then average the results.

Top Field Leaders (Top 10% Earners): Survey your highest performers on retention realities they observe in their teams.

New Participant Reality Check (0-90 Days): Anonymous feedback from recent customers and new reps on their experience and likelihood to continue.

Score Interpretation

8-10 Average per Section:

- **Healthy retention system.** Focus on optimization and scaling what works

- Continue monitoring trends and maintain current strategies

5-7 Average per Section:

- **Warning zone.** Retention leaks are costing you growth

- Address lowest-scoring areas immediately with focused 30-day tests

Below 5 Average per Section:

- **Crisis mode.** Culture is bleeding faster than you're building

- Halt new initiatives and focus entirely on plugging retention holes

Retention Recovery Action Plan

Start with your three lowest scores. Run 30-day tests on each gap. Track what actually moves the needle.:

Customer Retention Examples:

- Add personal check-in calls at days 7, 21, and 45

- Create customer-only Facebook group with exclusive content

- Implement win-back campaign for lapsed customers

Field Retention Examples:

- Launch 90-day new rep mentorship program

- Create mid-tier, company-wide recognition categories for consistent performers

- Add weekly activity scoreboards visible to team leaders

System Red Flag Examples:

- Separate customer and distributor communication sequences

- Train field leaders on retention metrics and tracking

- Shift 20% of event budget toward retention rewards

Step 3: Measure and Adjust Track improvement in your bottom 3 areas for 90 days. Scale what works, eliminate what doesn't.

Critical Success Factors

Retention is a leading indicator, not a lagging one. By the time you see declining enrollment numbers, you've already lost months of retention opportunities.

Warning Signs to Monitor Weekly:

- First-time customer reorder rates dropping below 40%

- New rep activity rates dropping below 30% at 60 days

- Increasing gap between corporate and field retention perceptions

- Recognition events celebrating volume over consistency

Remember: You can't growth-hack your way out of a retention crisis. Fix the experience, and the numbers will follow.

The Four-Month Loyalty Lock System

**The Four-Month Loyalty Lock:
When Customers Become Loyal**

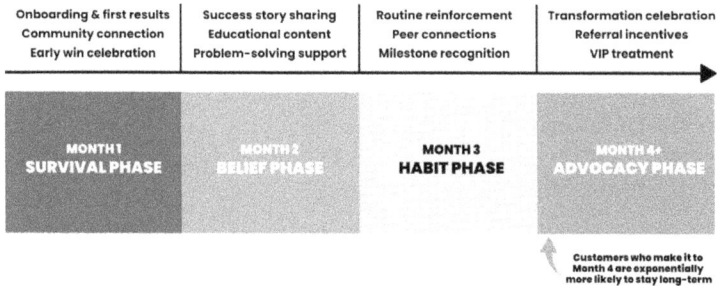

Onboarding & first results	Success story sharing	Routine reinforcement	Transformation celebration
Community connection	Educational content	Peer connections	Referral incentives
Early win celebration	Problem-solving support	Milestone recognition	VIP treatment
MONTH 1 **SURVIVAL PHASE**	**MONTH 2** **BELIEF PHASE**	**MONTH 3** **HABIT PHASE**	**MONTH 4+** **ADVOCACY PHASE**

Customers who make it to Month 4 are exponentially more likely to stay long-term

Engineer the journey. Don't hope for loyalty

Most companies track retention wrong. They look at annual numbers or monthly averages. But the real game is played in the first four months.

This framework works regardless of your product, price point, or current retention rates:

Step 1: Baseline Your Current Reality

Track your retention at these four critical checkpoints:

Month 1: Survival Phase

- Current retention rate: _____%

- Goal improvement: + _____%

- Focus: Onboarding, first results, community connection

Month 2: Belief Phase

- Current retention rate: _____%

- Goal improvement: + _____%

- Focus: Early wins, education, peer success stories

Month 3: Habit Phase

- Current retention rate: _____%

- Goal improvement: + _____%

- Focus: Routine building, deeper engagement, problem solving

Month 4: Advocacy Phase

- Current retention rate: _____%

- Goal improvement: + _____%

- Focus: Transformation stories, referrals, loyalty rewards

Step 2: Identify Your Biggest Drop-Off Point

Where do you lose the most customers? Between months 1-2? 2-3? 3-4?

That's your crisis point. That's where you engineer your fix first.

Crisis Point: Month ___ to Month ___
Current Drop-Off Rate: _____%
Target Improvement: _____%

Step 3: Build Phase-Specific Systems

For Survival Phase (Month 1):

- Welcome sequence (days 1, 3, 7, 14, 21, 30)

- First-use tutorial or coaching call

- Early win celebration (first reorder, first result, first share)

- Community introduction (customer group, app, forum)

For Belief Phase (Month 2):

- Success story sharing (customers like them)

- Educational content (how to maximize results)

- Check-in sequence (SMS, email, or call)

- Problem-solving support (common issues, solutions)

For Habit Phase (Month 3):

- Routine reinforcement (usage reminders, tips)

- Peer connection (buddy system, small groups)

- Milestone recognition (60-day member badge)

- Next-level education (advanced tips, exclusive content)

For Advocacy Phase (Month 4):

- Transformation celebration (before/after, testimonial)

- Referral incentives (friend discounts, bonuses)

- VIP treatment (exclusive access, special offers)

- Community leadership opportunities

Step 4: The Weekly Retention Scorecard

Track these metrics every week:

- New customers acquired this week: _____

- Month 1 retention rate: _____%

- Month 2 retention rate: _____%

- Month 3 retention rate: _____%

- Month 4+ retention rate: _____%

- Biggest drop-off point: Month ____ to Month ____

Step 5: Test And Optimize

Pick ONE phase to improve first. Run a 30-day test. Measure results. Then move to the next phase.

This Month's Focus: _____

Specific Change: _____

Target Improvement: + _____%

Actual Result: + _____%

What Actually Works For Customer Retention

Create dynamic onboarding flows based on what they bought. Not just welcome emails. Full sequences guiding customers through benefits, usage, expectations, and case studies. Progress check-ins at days 3, 10, 21. Think touch points, not broadcasts.

Segment your customer nurture paths. People who order once vs. subscribe vs. paused all need different messaging. Re-engage cancels with "We noticed you paused—here's why others came back." Educate single buyers on results that happen after months 2-3.

Track and test everything. You should know open rates, click-through rates, unsubscribe timing, which messages lead to reorders. Split test everything from subject lines to send times. If you can measure it, you can improve it.

Make customers feel seen, not sold. People stay based on emotion. They stay because they feel seen, valued, supported, understood, hopeful. SMS check-ins at 7, 21, and 45 days. Recognition emails: "We noticed you've been with us 60 days." Member-only training invites.

Build community around your product. If someone joins a customer group, retention increases. If they see success stories and human connection, they're 3x more likely to reorder. Make them feel like they're part of something built to last in direct selling.

How to Build the System With Your Field

Companies make the mistake of creating these systems in isolation.

Smart companies take a different approach: they co-create.

Form a committee. Bring your top field leaders together—the ones who are already getting people profitable fast. Add one or two corporate liaisons to support the process. Then step back.

Your job is to provide infrastructure, not interference. You facilitate. You coordinate. But you don't dictate.

Why? Because people commit to what they help create. And once that system is in place, you protect it. You track it. You keep it simple. You reinforce it with recognition and visibility.

The psychology matters more than the mechanics. When you help someone send that first message—even before they know exactly what to say—everything shifts. They go to bed thinking, "Maybe this could work." They imagine a friend trying the product. They wonder what it'd feel like to get their first customer. They start dreaming instead of doubting.

That changes everything. They're not going to bed with fears. They're going to bed with momentum.

Here's the ultimate test: Can a new builder explain in 30 seconds how they'll make back their initial investment? If not, your system isn't simple enough yet.

Statistically speaking, the longer a new rep goes without taking action, the less likely they are to ever get results. Think of it like an hourglass—you don't know how much sand is left, but you know the clock is running.

This is what turns potential into progress and when you build it with your field instead of for them, they'll protect it like they created it. Because they did.

You can't retain customers based on logic. People stay based on emotion.

Think of customer retention like reselling them on their decision to buy. Not with hype, but with proof.

If you can get customers to month 4, retention skyrockets. Your whole system should be reverse-engineered around this idea.

What happens at month 1 to keep them engaged? What do they feel after month 2? What extra support do they get at month 3? What reward can you deliver before month 4?

Customer retention isn't a finish line. It's a feedback loop.

You're never done optimizing. There's always a new tweak, a tighter message, a better customer journey.

If you want to grow faster, stop obsessing over acquisition. Start obsessing over the customers who already said yes.

They're your foundation. Your best future leaders. Your most powerful proof.

And if you treat them right, they'll stay. Not because they have to. But because they want to. In a profession fighting to rebuild trust, that's how you prove the model still works.

Recruiting is like pouring water into a bucket. Retention is whether or not that bucket has holes. Most companies obsess over how fast they're filling the bucket, but completely ignore how much is leaking out the bottom. You can't out-recruit bad retention forever. Fix the holes.

Retention creates the foundation. But retention without personal development just creates dependent customers. How do you turn retained customers into believers who grow as people? How do you create the emotional connection that makes people want to stay forever? That's where events come in. Because you can't describe a sunset—and you can't replace the power of being in the room.

Leadership development gives you the people. But retention gives you the foundation. Without both, you're teaching leaders to build on sand.

Retention keeps people in the game. But events make them believers. There's a difference between staying and belonging— and that difference changes everything.

CHAPTER 9

EVENTS

If you think a Zoom replay can replace the energy of a live event, you probably clap when planes land. Events aren't just meetings with better food, they're belief factories. If your events aren't driving retention, you're not hosting an experience—you're throwing an expensive party.

You can't describe a sunset.

Not really.

You can try. You'll say the colors were unbelievable, the water shimmered, and the air felt electric. But no matter how good you are with words, you'll fall short.

That's how it is with events.

You had to be there.

Try explaining your favorite concert to someone who wasn't there. What do you say? "The ambiance was amazing"? "The crowd was into it"?

That doesn't land. You had to feel it. You had to live it.

This is exactly what most corporate teams miss when they treat in-person events as optional, outdated, or interchangeable with Zooms.

Virtual can support, but it cannot replace. You don't build movement on replays. You build movement in the room.

Events are everything.

They bring together every major thread we've talked about in this book—culture, leadership development, recognition, momentum, belief, vision, community.

If you want a business built to last in direct selling, events can't be your afterthought. They have to be your anchor.

TED Talks proved the power of being in the room.

TED started as a small conference in 1984—technology, entertainment, design. Nothing fancy. But something magical happened when brilliant minds gathered in one space. The energy was infectious. Ideas sparked ideas. Conversations continued long after speakers left the stage.

By 2006, TED videos were going viral online. Millions of views. Global reach. But here's what's interesting: despite having the world's best content available free online, people still pay thousands to attend TED live. The waitlist is years long. Why? Because watching a TED talk and experiencing TED are completely different things.

The ideas are the same. The impact isn't.

Being in the room with 1,400 people who are all leaning forward, all thinking bigger, all believing more—that's what changes you. The video informs you. The event transforms you.

The same principle applies in network marketing: people don't attend events for information—they attend for transformation. They want to see who they could become. They want to feel capable of more than they thought possible. Your product or opportunity might get them to register, but personal transformation is what gets them to implement. The best events don't just teach what to do—they help people believe they can do it.

Lesson: Events are the heartbeat of a direct selling company. But that heartbeat only stays strong when the field helps set the rhythm. Lose that connection, and even the biggest gathering will feel empty. Get it right, and you'll build something that lasts—because your people will feel like they belong.

Most companies treat events like a logistical headache.

Booked last minute. Promoted weakly. Budgeted defensively. Streamed like a checkbox.

But events aren't just "a thing we do." Events are a core product of belief.

Your actual product gets someone to buy. Your event gets someone to believe.

That belief doesn't just happen in the general session. It happens in the hotel lobby at midnight, when three strangers swap breakthrough stories and end up in each other's weddings two years later. It happens at the breakfast table, when a brand-new rep hears a 60-year-old mom talk about paying off her mortgage from a side hustle she almost quit. It happens in the back row, when someone hears a leader who sounds like them, thinks like them, and looks like them—and says, "If they did it, maybe I can."

None of that translates to Zoom. Zoom can supplement education. But events multiply belief.

People are hungry for real. They're starving for connection.

People are starving for connection. They want a room. They want to feel something again.

Events aren't just strategic. They're human.

Try explaining your best vacation. I went to Bora Bora once. Unbelievable place. But how do I explain the nine shades of turquoise in the ocean? The stillness of the air? The way the sunset just swallowed the sky?

You can't. You had to be there.

Same with concerts. You don't relive your favorite concert through someone's phone recording. You remember the moment the beat dropped, and the whole room exploded.

Events are that moment.

The Best Companies Don't Just Host Events. They Scale Them.

One Major Flagship Event Per Year Not optional. Not virtual. Not diluted. This is your Super Bowl. Your linchpin. Your culture cement. Every team builds for it. Everything aligns with it.

Leadership Retreats with Built-in Development Don't just wine and dine the top reps. Build in private Q&As. Bring in outside trainers who can stretch their vision. Add strategy rooms. Make them earn it.

Rank-Specific Experiences Fly in new top ranks for one-day intensives. Extend convention by a day for leadership cohorts. Host pre-convention executive previews. Scale mentorship by design, not luck.

Team Ownership at Events Every leader should feel like a host, not a guest. Provide toolkits for team dinners, recognition meetups, coffee chats. The host gets the most.

Teaching Your Field To Own Events

Train your leaders how to promote events like a launch. Teach countdowns, previews, VIP bonuses, roadmaps. Recognize event attendance—spotlight leaders with the most reps attending. Show them how to run team breakouts. Even 5-person breakfasts matter. Culture is built in circles, not stadiums.

Build traditions. Consistent room blocks. Colors. Dinners. Hashtags. Small details become big memories.

Stop streaming your main event. You think you're helping people "stay plugged in." You're actually giving them a reason to stay home, and most of them won't even watch. They'll "mean to" and never will.

If you must do digital, create post-event summary series. Highlight reels. Panel interviews. Clips with calls to action. But don't replace the fire. Make them want it.

Create an annual events roadmap. Plan a full 12 months ahead. Partner with leaders—don't just talk at them. Co-create with your field's top voices. Train your field to promote, not just hype. Measure what

151

matters: Who brings the most guests? What's the attendance-to-rank correlation?

Stop assuming they'll show up. You have to sell them on being there.

Because when they are—They won't just remember the speeches. They'll remember the moment they finally believed again, and belief is what this profession needs to rebuild trust—one person at a time.

Events build belief at home. But what happens when you want to take that belief global? Most companies think international expansion is just copy-and-paste. They're wrong. This is why most companies fail before they even launch overseas.

Retention keeps people in the game, but events make them believers. There's a difference between staying and belonging—and that difference changes everything.

How Corporate Can Build Event Momentum by Understanding What Actually Works

Most corporate teams think event promotion means sending announcements and hoping for the best. That's why attendance is inconsistent and energy fades between events.

Smart companies understand the mechanics of field-driven event promotion—not to micromanage it, but to support it. When corporate knows what actually drives attendance, they can create systems that amplify field efforts instead of competing with them.

Here's what your best field leaders are already doing (and how corporate can support each phase):

Event Promotion Framework Your Field Leaders Need (*Corporate can provide templates and tools for each step*)

Phase 1: Foundation Building (30-60 Days Out) *Top field leaders start by identifying their core promoters—their natural influencers who others follow. Corporate can support this by providing:*

- *Recognition programs that spotlight these key promoters*

- *Early access or VIP perks for leaders who commit to driving attendance*

- *Attendance tracking tools that make it easy for leaders to set team goals*

Field leaders create weekly touch points—Zooms, team chats, social posts—that build event anticipation. Corporate enables this by:

- *Providing shareable content leaders can customize*

- *Creating video testimonial templates from previous events*

- *Funding small contest prizes (hotel upgrades, VIP experiences) leaders can use.*

The smartest companies help field leaders remove logistics barriers:

- *Facilitate carpool and hotel-sharing coordination*

- *Provide early bird pricing that creates urgency*

- *Offer payment plans that make attendance accessible*

Phase 2: Final Week Intensity *This is where momentum either accelerates or stalls. Field leaders need corporate support to:*

- *Access final attendance numbers to create team accountability*

- *Get last-minute promotional materials that address common objections*

- *Coordinate with corporate for any final incentives or upgrades*

Phase 3: The Most Critical 48 Hours—During the Event *Here's what most corporate teams miss:* your best promotional window isn't before the event—it's during it.

Top field leaders know to promote the next event while attendees are emotionally peak. But they need corporate coordination:

- Next event dates and early pricing ready to announce

- Registration systems that work seamlessly during high-traffic moments

- Recognition tools (colored lanyards, stage shoutouts, social graphics) for immediate commitments

Corporate should expect and plan for this sales window. Your highest conversion rates happen when belief is highest—right in the room.

Phase 4: Post-Event Momentum Capture The 48-72 hours after an event determine whether momentum carries forward or dies. Field leaders who understand this run:

- Immediate recap calls to solidify commitments

- Action plan sessions that turn inspiration into activity

- Social campaigns that extend the event energy

Corporate can support this critical phase by providing:

- Post-event follow-up templates and frameworks

- Tools that help leaders track and measure post-event activity

- Recognition systems for leaders who effectively capture momentum

How Corporate Should Recognize Event Builders Recognition creates replication. When corporate celebrates the right behaviors, more leaders adopt them:

- Track and spotlight leaders who bring the most new attendees

- Provide special recognition during events (VIP seating, backstage access)

- Feature top promoters in corporate communications

- Create annual awards for leaders who consistently drive attendance

What Corporate Teams Should Understand About Event Impact

Field leaders know these truths about live events, but corporate often underestimates them. When you understand what actually happens at events, you'll invest differently in making them happen:

The Real Reasons People Need to Be in the Room:

- New connections spark new belief—relationships form that sustain people through tough months.

- Confidence grows in the environment, not in comfort zones—people discover capabilities they didn't know they had.

- It creates productive FOMO for everyone watching from sidelines—non-attendees see what they missed.

- Events remind people why they started—vision gets rekindled when daily grind has dulled it.

- It deepens loyalty and connection to the team—shared experiences bond people differently than virtual interactions.

- Leaders are born at events—people step up when surrounded by others stepping up.

- Breakthroughs happen when you're fully immersed—removing distractions creates mental space for growth.

- People move from dabbling to deciding—events force commitment decisions that change trajectories.

- Events are belief factories—skepticism melts when you see real people with real results.

- If leaders aren't there, their teams see it and copy it—attendance becomes culture from the top down.

This isn't motivational theory—it's business reality. Corporate teams that understand these dynamics invest in events differently. They fund them properly. They measure the right metrics. They remove barriers instead of creating them.

Because when you know what events actually accomplish, you stop treating them as expenses and start treating them as engines.

5 Non-Negotiables For Events That Drive Belief

1. **No streaming the main event**. Make attendance matter. Look, streaming can work if you understand the trade-offs. You'll reach

more people but create less urgency. You'll get broader access but weaker commitment. Most companies stream because it feels inclusive, but what they're really doing is training people that being there doesn't matter. For your biggest annual event—the one that sets the tone for everything—make attendance the only way to experience it. Create productive FOMO, not convenient excuses.

2. **Field leaders co-create content**. Don't lecture at them Your top builders know what the field needs to hear better than your marketing team does. Let them shape agendas, suggest speakers, and run breakout sessions. When leaders feel like hosts instead of guests, they promote harder and show up bigger.

3. **Recognition reflects reality**. Not just the elite If your stage time only goes to million-dollar earners, you've lost everyone else. Celebrate the consistent, the comeback stories, the quiet builders. Make sure your recognition shows the field who they can become, not just who they'll never be.

4. **Follow-up systems.** Capture momentum in 48 hours The most critical sales window isn't before your event—it's during and immediately after. Have systems ready to capture commitments, register new goals, and channel inspiration into action. Momentum has a shelf life. Use it or lose it.

5. **Create the full emotional spectrum through personal development.** Make them feel everything while they grow. Your audience has Netflix, TikTok, and Taylor Swift concerts competing for their attention. They expect to be entertained, not just informed. But entertainment without transformation is just expensive theater. Great events weave personal development throughout—making people laugh at breakthrough stories, cry at transformation moments, then feel inspired to become better humans. Share

the journey, not just the destination. The single mom who built confidence while building her business. The introvert who found their voice. The couple who saved their marriage while building their team. If someone leaves your event feeling the same as when they walked in, you failed. Events that help people grow as humans create loyalty that outlasts any comp plan change.

The Business Case for Field-Driven Event Promotion When field leaders own event promotion with corporate support:

- Attendance becomes sustainable, not dependent on corporate push

- Events become leadership development opportunities for promoters

- Teams develop stronger internal accountability and culture

- Corporate resources get leveraged through field multiplication

Your role isn't to promote events—it's to make field promotion easier, more effective, and more rewarding. When you do that, attendance becomes self-sustaining and events become true culture builders.

The companies with the strongest event cultures don't just host great events—they develop leaders who create an appetite for the next one.

Events build belief at home when you understand what drives attendance and create systems that support field-driven promotion. But what happens when you want to take that belief global? Most companies think international expansion is just copy-and-paste events in different languages. They're wrong. That's why most companies fail before they even launch overseas.

.

If you're launching internationally with Google Translate and prayer, you're not expanding—you're gambling. And the house always wins. Every 'fake opening' makes it harder for legitimate companies to gain trust in that market. Here's how to expand like you mean it.

CHAPTER 10

INTERNATIONAL EXPANSION

You can create powerful events that build unshakeable belief. But that belief means nothing if you can't scale it responsibly across borders.

The fastest way to lose credibility in a global market? Show up without real intent.

There's an epidemic right now of what I call "fake openings." A North American company launches in another country—not because they're ready, not because they've committed—but because they're praying that market takes off and saves their quarterly revenue.

No market wants to be someone's hope and a prayer, and frankly they've stopped tolerating it.

A fake opening looks like this: No in-country general manager with decision-making authority. No localized packaging, language, or promotional materials. No country-specific onboarding or customer experience flow. No serious efforts made to register products legally. No customer service in time zones that actually serve the market. No long-term leadership development plan for the region. No boots-on-the-ground investment — just fly-ins, hype, and translation.

It's a drive-by launch, and the field knows it. Why should they go all in when the company clearly hasn't?

3 NON-NEGOTIABLES BEFORE YOU LAUNCH INTERNATIONAL

If you're about to announce a new country, stop. Don't post the flag. Don't book the hotel, and for the love of credibility, don't send your US leaders to "build it out" before you've handled these three things:

1. **Price points and product bundles built for that market** What's affordable in the U.S. might be luxury pricing overseas. Don't just convert currency. Build real bundles that make sense for how people shop, what they can afford, and how they prefer to buy. Every product line needs a starter option—and an irresistible upgrade path. If they can't buy smart, they won't buy at all.

2. **Comp plan customized for the economy and culture** Direct sales reps in Brazil don't build the same way as leaders in Germany or Thailand. If your comp plan doesn't reflect local behaviors, it's just a foreign-language math problem. Rework the thresholds. Adjust the fast-starts. Make sure your incentives actually reward activity that's realistic for that market.

3. **Field-driven belief built before the ribbon-cutting** The field needs to believe in the launch before you announce it, not after. Seed the market. Get product in hands. Start telling stories *inside* that country, not just about it. No one wants to be the first customer.

They want to be part of something that's already working. Create belief before you create buzz.

Stop Obsessing Over What You're Missing. Maximize What You've Got.

Why do companies make fake openings? Because they're always chasing what they don't have instead of maximizing what they've got.

Old companies want to feel young again. Young companies want the credibility of age. Female-dominated companies want more men. Male-dominated companies want more women. Latino markets want to crack the U.S. U.S. based companies want to explode internationally.

It never ends. Companies always want what they don't have.

While it's fine to diversify, the fastest way to scale is to double down on what's working. That means putting more resources, attention, and momentum behind your core strengths—not distracting the team with constant identity pivots.

Yes, aim for strategic growth. Yes, shore up weak spots. But don't turn your entire vision upside down just to chase validation in an area that wasn't yours to win in the first place.

If you've got a community that's thriving in one demo, age group, or region, expand there first. Build your fortress before you try to build an empire.

You don't need to become something you're not. You just need to own what you are—louder.

International expansion works when it's an extension of domestic strength, not an escape from domestic problems.

International teams are growing weary of being treated like beta testers. They've seen too many launches fizzle after six months. They've heard the promises, watched the promotions, and been burned by the silence when the company realizes it costs real money and time to build something sustainable.

You don't get loyalty from a region you're not loyal to.

IKEA's American launch was an unmitigated disaster that almost killed their global expansion dreams.

In 1985, IKEA opened their first U.S. store outside Philadelphia with supreme confidence. They had conquered Europe with their Swedish formula—why wouldn't Americans love affordable, minimalist furniture? Within the first month, customers were walking in, laughing out loud, and walking straight back out. The beds were sized for Europeans—too small for American standards. Everything was measured in centimeters when Americans thought in feet and inches. The kitchen cabinets didn't fit standard American appliances. Even the meatballs in their café were European-style recipes that American palates rejected. Sales were so catastrophically low that internal projections showed they'd burn through their entire U.S. investment within eighteen months.

This wasn't just poor performance—this was a company watching its global expansion strategy collapse in real-time, with board members in Sweden questioning whether IKEA could ever succeed outside Europe.

IKEA made the painful decision to completely rebuild their American operation from scratch. They redesigned beds to American king and queen sizes. They converted every measurement to inches and feet. They reformulated their food offerings for American tastes. They hired American suppliers and invested $1.5 billion in U.S. based manufacturing. Most importantly, they hired American managers who understood local customer behavior and gave them authority to make regional decisions without checking with Sweden first.

Today, IKEA operates 52 stores across America generating over $5 billion in annual U.S. revenue. They've successfully expanded to 63 countries worldwide, with total global revenue exceeding $47 billion. Their willingness to adapt rather than force their original model became the blueprint for every subsequent international expansion.

IKEA adapts or it doesn't bother showing up. Local wins. Arrogance loses.

For direct selling, this is the expansion playbook: Adapt to the market. Hire local. Listen more than you talk. Kill what isn't working. Or get ready to pack up and go home.

Agel: When Going Wide Without Depth Led to Collapse

Agel Enterprises launched in March 2005, shipping its first Suspension Gel Technology products just two months later. With a founder who'd spent nearly two decades in network marketing, Agel's ambition was global from day one. By early 2007—less than two years in—they were already operating in over 20 countries, including the US, Australia, Canada, and throughout Europe and Asia. By 2010, they'd opened a new corporate headquarters in Pleasant Grove, Utah, and claimed millions of gel packs sold with tens of thousands of distributors worldwide.

The vision was everywhere, fast. Within 24 months, Agel was doing over $1 million a month in five different countries. The field was buzzing, and the hype was real. But beneath the surface, cracks were already forming. Local teams in many countries became "orphans"— they had no real corporate support, no consistent training, and no compliance oversight. Distributors in new markets reported late bonus payments, supply chain breakdowns, and months-long waits for basic communication from headquarters. In some regions, product shipments were delayed for weeks, leaving teams with nothing to sell and no answers for customers. Leadership turnover became common, and local leaders were left to fend for themselves.

By 2014, the warning signs were everywhere: field complaints about late commissions, patchy customer service, and rumors of financial instability. Agel's global infrastructure simply couldn't keep up with the pace of expansion. In 2015, Agel was acquired by JRJR Networks, a company known for buying struggling direct sellers. The hope was to stabilize operations and fix the supply chain, but the damage was already done. By 2016, Agel's field engagement and sales had declined sharply. Many markets lost most of their active distributors within a year. Reports of late payments and leadership turnover accelerated the exodus, and Agel's once-global footprint shrank almost as quickly as it had grown.

The lesson is clear: Agel's story isn't just about rapid growth—it's about what happens when you go wide without going deep. Orphaned teams, broken infrastructure, and a lack of compliance turned global momentum into a global collapse. Focus and depth beat speed and breadth every time.

Most companies refuse to face this reality: How many direct sales companies actually do over $1 million a month in more than 5 different countries?

If you're a veteran in this industry, you know the answer. They're few and far between. Teams fluctuate, companies give different numbers, but when you strip away the marketing and look at sustained, consistent performance across multiple markets—the list gets very short, very fast.

Yet every company thinks they're going to be the exception. They skip the fundamentals, burn through their reserves trying to look global, and wonder why nothing sticks.

The billion-dollar dream is seductive. But most companies chase it backwards. They try to look like a billion-dollar company before they've built the foundation of a sustainable hundred-million-dollar one. They spread thin instead of building deep. They prioritize expansion over retention, and they run out of money before they run out of countries to disappoint.

International doesn't mean easier growth.

Yes, international can create leverage. While one market is soft, another can carry revenue. But international also means expensive legal approvals, ongoing compliance regulation, currency fluctuation risks, product delays, high support costs, different cultural values and market maturity, the risk of losing focus at home.

Some countries require proof of capital reserves to open. Others require specific product formulations or ingredient bans, and many require full physical infrastructure or serious partnerships to go legit.

If you're not fully ready — don't fake it. Because once a market has lost trust, it doesn't come back easy.

Launching a country is like releasing a movie.

If it doesn't go well opening weekend, it often never gains traction. A great launch doesn't guarantee long-term success. But a bad launch almost always guarantees failure.

A great launch doesn't mean you hype it up for a month, ship a few orders, and hope a top leader moves there. A great launch looks like: fully localized website and back office, real-time translated support, local leadership calls, regulatory compliance and approval, custom promos that show you know their economy and customer.

You only get one first impression in a new country. Treat it like it matters.

The three mistakes most companies make:

1. They expand too soon. Momentum in one market makes corporate greedy. They get excited, then distracted, then stretched thin. Now their current teams feel ignored and the new market feels underserved.

2. They don't understand the real cost. You're not just translating PDFs — you're navigating laws, hiring legal experts, registering products, managing logistics, and dealing with real currency and taxation challenges.

3. They don't know the culture. You can't cut and paste your U.S. strategy into Asia, Europe, or Latin America. Every country has different motivators, skepticism levels, buying patterns, and leadership styles.

Real commitment looks different than corporate thinks.

You want to win globally? Prove it. In-country general managers with real field trust. Localized customer service with culturally aligned hours. Custom promotional strategies designed for each region. Translated tools and onboarding experiences. Consistent in-market events — not just Zooms from HQ. Clear registration of products with local authorities. Physical infrastructure plans. Dedicated marketing, legal, and compliance attention. Structured leader development systems, not just deals. Fair, custom compensation that fits economics of the region.

You want leaders to treat your company like home? Then act like you're moving in.

When it's done right, international markets become one of your greatest assets.

Because when one market dips, another rises. You create balance, diversity, and economic durability. But only if each country is built with care, not copied and pasted built to last in direct selling.

Your international strategy should be measured not by how many markets you're in…but by how well the people in those markets trust your commitment.

The best companies expand internationally with intention. Not because they need a revenue band-aid. But because they're building something worth multiplying.

Legacy companies don't just show up in countries—they embed. They create multi-language platforms. They hire for cultural fluency. They stop relying on U.S. leaders to "build it over there" and start raising leadership within the region.

Legacy companies know this is more than market share—it's a relationship. And relationships require trust, respect, and follow-through.

International Launch Readiness Checklist

Before you even think about announcing a new market, run this diagnostic. The difference between a successful launch and an expensive disaster often comes down to preparation, not excitement.

Rate each item 1–10 (1 = not ready, 10 = fully prepared):

- ☐ Local GM hired with cultural and operational authority
- ☐ Product offerings tailored for local regulations, preferences, and demand
- ☐ Comp plan adapted to market behavior, not copy-pasted
- ☐ Translation/localization tested with real reps, not just Google Translate
- ☐ In-country pre-launch event secured with top leader involvement
- ☐ Fulfillment + customer service fully operational locally
- ☐ Leadership pre-load plan (local leaders + natives of that market mapped and engaged)
- ☐ Launch content localized (videos, onboarding, presentations)
- ☐ Field-facing FAQ prepped in local language with real objections
- ☐ 12–24 month commitment plan clearly communicated internally and externally

Final Score: ___/100

Readiness Assessment:

- **80–100:** Launch-ready. You've done the work.

- **60–79:** Caution zone—refine strategy before announcing.

- **Below 60:** Delay launch. You're not ready, and the market will know it.

Remember: It's better to launch one country right than three countries wrong. The field talks across borders faster than you think.

Global Expansion Playbook

Practical Strategies for International Growth in Direct Sales

Most companies treat international expansion like domestic growth with translation. That's why most fail. Here's what actually works when you're serious about building globally:

1. Decentralize Marketing Efforts

Empower local leaders and reps to adapt messaging for their culture. Avoid corporate bottlenecks that slow everything down. Build duplicable systems anyone can teach, but let them customize the delivery for local relevance.

Reality Check: Your American success story might not resonate in Germany. Let your German leaders find German success stories.

2. Leverage Local Technology

Use the right platforms for each market—Facebook Groups work in some regions, WhatsApp dominates others. LINE in Japan, WeChat in China, Telegram in Eastern Europe. Don't force your preferred platform on markets that live elsewhere.

Back it with real infrastructure: Multi-currency systems, local tax compliance, seamless translation, and CRM visibility that works across time zones.

3. Respect Culture And Law

Customize packaging, messaging, and product selection for local preferences and regulations. Hire local legal counsel—not just translators of your U.S. legal documents. Build in cultural nuance from day one.

Truth: What works in Kansas won't work in Kuala Lumpur, and that's not a problem to solve—it's a reality to embrace.

4. Mix Your Market Entry Strategy

Use direct sales where you have relationship-driven leadership with proven track records. Use channel partners or importers in markets with higher barriers or lower field maturity. APAC and LATAM often require hybrid approaches.

Don't force the same entry strategy in every market just because it's easier for corporate to manage.

5. Nail The Logistics First

If your shipping, customs, and return process isn't predictable, nothing else matters. Work with regional logistics experts before you commit to a launch date. Test the entire fulfillment cycle with real orders, not just samples.

Non-Negotiable: Your international customers deserve the same experience as your domestic ones. If you can't deliver that, don't launch.

6. Over Invest In Training

Daily training. Step-by-step duplication. Local-language onboarding that actually works. Global growth doesn't mean complicated—it means duplicated successfully across cultures.

Train your trainers first. Give them tools that work in their language, their culture, their time zone. Don't just translate your U.S. training—recreate it for local success.

7. Lead With Community

Products may start conversations, but people stay for connection. Attend field-led events, recognize builders early, and act like a partner—not an owner extracting value.

Build relationships before you build revenue. The field will forgive mistakes if they trust your intentions.

8. Stay Agile

Global expansion is speed over perfection, but not recklessness over preparation. Test fast. Learn fast. Adjust faster.

Don't let your field outrun your ability to support them. And don't let corporate perfectionism slow down market momentum.

The Bottom Line: International expansion isn't about how many flags you can put on your website. It's about how many markets genuinely trust you to be there for the long haul.

Build trust first. Revenue follows.

International expansion tests every system you've built. But even the best global strategy falls apart if your infrastructure can't support it. Most companies obsess over the shiniest tech stack while their field struggles with basics. Because if your tools are so good that your team doesn't talk to people anymore, you didn't build a system— you built a crutch.

You can create powerful events that build unshakeable belief. But that belief means nothing if you can't scale it responsibly across borders.

International expansion reveals every weakness in your foundation. But infrastructure problems don't wait for you to go global—they kill momentum at home first. When I say infrastructure, I'm not talking about just software or IT systems—I'm talking about the invisible frameworks that support culture, communication, compliance, and scalability. The operational backbone that determines whether growth strengthens your foundation or cracks it.

CHAPTER 11

INFRASTRUCTURE AND TOOLS

If your tools are so good that your team doesn't talk to people anymore, you didn't build a system — you built a crutch.

There's nothing wrong with great infrastructure. The problem is when infrastructure starts replacing initiative.

That's the trap a lot of network marketing companies fall into. They think the next CRM, AI bot, or training portal is going to be the thing that turns the tide.

But it never is; because the tool isn't the magic, the distributor is.

The tool is the key. But the distributor is the hand that picks it up, turns the lock, opens the door, and invites someone in.

The Infrastructure-Culture Balance: When Tools Become Crutches

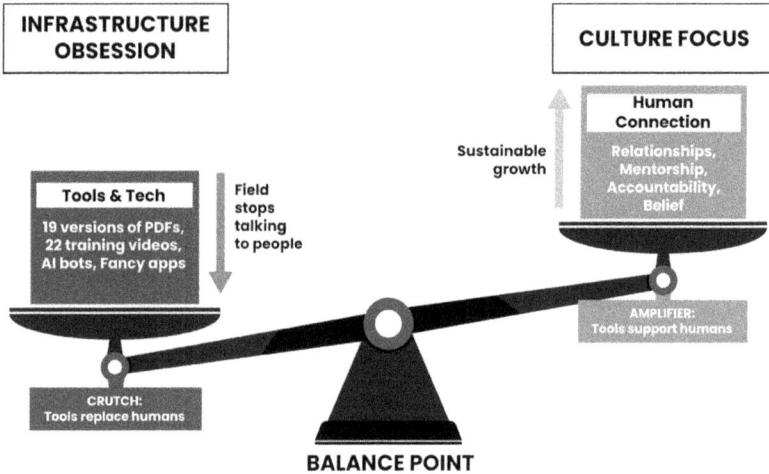

INFRASTRUCTURE OBSESSION

CULTURE FOCUS

Human Connection

Relationships, Mentorship, Accountability, Belief

Sustainable growth

Tools & Tech

19 versions of PDFs, 22 training videos, AI bots, Fancy apps

Field stops talking to people

AMPLIFIER: Tools support humans

CRUTCH: Tools replace humans

BALANCE POINT

Infrastructure should amplify what humans do well, not replace what humans do best.

When you make the key look flashy, but forget about the hand, you lose the human element. You end up with amazing tech and disappointing growth.

Too many companies make the mistake of over-developing infrastructure and under-developing behavior.

A well-designed tool should support what already works — not try to make up for what doesn't.

What companies get wrong: They create nineteen versions of a PDF but can't explain the first step to a new rep. They film twenty two training videos before teaching anyone how to actually invite. They build AI-generated onboarding journeys with no human follow-up. They invest six figures into apps and zero dollars into leadership development.

The result? A fancy shell, but no heartbeat. And without consistent human connection, no system scales sustainably.

Toyota: When Empowerment Beat the Odds

In the early 1980s, Toyota's U.S. plants were a mess. Defects were everywhere—one out of every twenty cars rolled off the line with a major problem. Production was slow, waste was rampant, and Toyota was getting trounced by the Detroit Big Three. American executives dismissed Toyota's approach as too rigid, too foreign, and too idealistic for U.S. workers. The conflict? Toyota had to prove their system could work in a skeptical, resistant culture—or risk being written off as just another failed import experiment.

So Toyota bet everything on the Toyota Production System (TPS). This wasn't just a new process—it was a revolution. Every worker, from the newest hire to the most senior manager, was given the authority to stop the entire production line if they spotted a defect. It was called the "andon cord." Pull it, and the whole plant stopped. In Detroit, that was unthinkable. In Toyota's world, it was non-negotiable.

While Detroit managers hoarded control and blamed workers for problems, Toyota handed out real power. The philosophy of Kaizen—continuous improvement—became the heartbeat of every plant. Workers submitted thousands of improvement suggestions every year. Management listened. They didn't just hand out manuals; they handed out real authority. The result? Within five years, Toyota's U.S. plants cut defects by 50%. Productivity soared—by the early 1990s, Toyota was building cars in Kentucky faster and with fewer errors than any plant in Detroit. By 1997, Toyota's U.S. plants outperformed the Big Three on every metric: quality, speed, and cost. Market share doubled. The rest of the industry was forced to adapt or die.

For direct selling, this isn't just a story about cars—it's a blueprint for infrastructure that actually works. Give your people the tools, the authority, and the responsibility to fix problems in real time. Don't just hand out rulebooks—hand out real power. When your field has that power, your business doesn't just run. It thrives.

United Sciences of America: The Orphan Factory

United Sciences of America (USA) exploded onto the scene in January 1986, promising to revolutionize nutrition with "cutting-edge science" and a star-studded advisory board. The hype was off the charts: William Shatner narrated their recruitment videos, and sports legends like Chris Evert and Gary Carter endorsed the products. Within seven months, USA signed up 140,000 distributors—adding 10,000 to 15,000 new reps every month. Executives boasted of $8 million in revenue in 1986 and projected $100 million that year, with a billion-dollar target by 1989. The company's "Master Formula" and other products were marketed as miracle solutions for everything from cancer to heart disease.

But the foundation was hollow. USA built for growth, not support. There was no real onboarding—new reps got a $24.50 "Success System Kit" and a VHS tape, but little else. Customer service was overwhelmed and often unreachable. There were no real systems for field follow-up, training, or compliance. As the field ballooned, cracks turned into chasms. Distributors flooded the company with questions and complaints, but got no answers. Many went months without a single call or email from corporate. By late 1986, thousands of reps were "orphans"—signed up, but with no support, no training, and no hope of success.

The collapse was dramatic and public. In October 1986, NBC aired a devastating exposé revealing fraudulent scientific claims and misleading endorsements. In November, commission payments stopped. By December, checks to distributors were bouncing. By

January 1987, the FDA and attorneys general in California, New York, and Texas were investigating the company for false advertising and pyramid scheme tactics. Several scientific advisors resigned, accusing USA of misusing their names. In April 1987, just 15 months after launch, USA filed for Chapter 7 bankruptcy with $8.6 million in debt and 140,000 distributors completely abandoned.

USA proves the point: infrastructure isn't about looking big, it's about supporting the people you have. Build for hype, and you'll leave a trail of orphans. Build for support, and you might actually last.

The danger isn't just poor infrastructure—it's infrastructure that can't scale with momentum. Too many companies build systems for where they are, not where they're going.

You absolutely need tools. You need onboarding tools. You need training frameworks. You need back office reports. You need systems.

What You Actually Need vs. What Just Looks Good in a Slide Deck

What You Actually Need:

- A getting-started system that drives first action in 24 hours

- Tools that help reps invite, follow up, and duplicate faster

- Scorecards that track behavior — not just clicks and logins

- Simple content reps can explain without needing slides

- A system rhythm the field can repeat weekly without guessing

- Tech that reinforces leadership — not tries to replace it

- AI that supports action — not replaces connection

What Just Looks Good in a Slide Deck:

- 40 apps with 47 features nobody asked for

- AI bots that confuse more than they clarify

- Dashboards built to impress corporate, not drive field action

- Tools that require 6 videos to explain and still don't duplicate

- Ideas that sound brilliant but never get implemented

- Branding projects that look good but slow down execution

But you need them to scale leadership, not replace it.

Tools are there to create consistency. To simplify duplication. To reduce overwhelm. But they only work when they're part of a larger ecosystem built on action and belief.

The best tools amplify what humans do well. They don't replace what humans do best.

Think of the best companies you've seen in momentum. The ones that grew like wildfire. Were they known for elaborate, overbuilt tool stacks? No.

They kept it simple. Their systems made sense. They had rhythm. Predictability. Urgency. Speed. Their tools didn't try to do the work for the field. They enabled the work.

The most important part of creating any tool is teaching people how to actually use it.

This is where most companies fail. They build something incredible, launch it with fanfare, then wonder why adoption is terrible and results don't improve.

You can have the world's best CRM, but if your team doesn't know how to track prospects or follow up consistently, it's just expensive software taking up space.

You can build the most sophisticated onboarding app, but if new reps don't understand how to plug people into it and guide them through it, you've just created a fancy way for people to get overwhelmed and quit.

Tools can be your greatest strength or your greatest weakness. The difference is whether you treat them as force multipliers or force replacers.

Training should always come back to two things: How fast can someone take their first action? How well can they duplicate that with someone else?

This is why scorecards matter. This is why daily and weekly actions matter. This is why your systems need to reinforce momentum — not slow it down.

If your "tool" takes 90 minutes to explain, it's not a tool. It's a roadblock. If your training has 27 modules before someone learns how to invite, it's not a training. It's a distraction.

Great systems help people win faster. That's it.

Nu Skin: When Success Bred Complexity

Remember Nu Skin's North American turnaround? The Galvanic Spa demo that rebuilt belief and drove sales from $220.1 million in 2007 to $262.0 million in 2008?

That momentum kept rolling. By 2012, North American sales hit $300.1 million. The field was energized. Leadership was confident. Success had a way of making you believe you'd cracked the code.

So they decided to accelerate.

2013 brought the ageLOC TR90 weight management program—an internally developed system with nutritional supplements, meal replacement shakes, and structured eating plans. Complex protocols, multiple components, and premium pricing. Sales ticked up to $310.5 million. The strategy seemed validated.

But something else was happening beneath the surface. The same company that had saved itself with simplicity was now drowning its own story in options. The napkin-simple Galvanic demo became one choice among many. Field leaders who once carried a single device were now juggling multiple product lines, each with its own training, certification, and messaging.

The five-minute demo that rebuilt belief? It disappeared under layers of choice and complexity. What used to duplicate effortlessly now required detailed explanations.

Leonardo da Vinci said simplicity is the ultimate sophistication. Nu Skin had mastered sophistication and abandoned simplicity. It doesn't matter how good your changes are—when you make too many of them too fast, they always end up bad. And in network marketing, what works is what duplicates. Confusion kills momentum.

The numbers tell the story. 2014: $305.0 million. 2015: $295.0 million. 2016: $285.0 million. By 2017, North American sales had retreated to $275.0 million—$35 million below peak and heading in the wrong direction.

It wasn't product failure. It was narrative drift. They had taken the simple story that saved them and made it complicated again.

Nu Skin remains a powerhouse today, but their stumble proves even the best companies can lose their way. Success has a way of making you forget the fundamentals. Pro golfers warm up with three-foot putts while amateurs start from twenty feet. NBA stars begin every practice with layups while weekend warriors launch threes. Tennis pros start rallying from the service line while club players swing for winners from the baseline.

Successful people and companies just do the basics better. But with success, most forget this lesson and need to be reminded to return to the basics.

The field didn't need more products—they needed the company to remember what made them great: giving people something they could duplicate, not just admire. When you build infrastructure that complicates instead of simplifies, you don't just slow growth—you reverse it.

The best corporate teams build tools that are plug-and-play. Simple enough for a brand-new rep to use on Day 1. Field-tested with top leaders who actually use them—not just corporate strategy teams. Every tool maps directly to a specific income-producing activity. They work across markets and leadership styles. Usage is tracked, funnel points are clear, action is measured.

These companies separate tool creation from tool worship. They don't obsess over the next launch or platform. They obsess over field usability.

Is it being used? Is it driving results? Is it creating real momentum? Is it simple enough to explain in sixty seconds? If the answer is no — they change it.

There are two ways companies mess this up:

They overspend too early. Fancy offices. Too many VPs. Huge marketing contracts. Massive backend tech stacks that barely get used. They start operating like they're a billion-dollar brand before they've even stabilized retention.

Or they underspend in the wrong areas. No real customer support system. A back office that breaks with volume. A rep portal that confuses instead of converts. Zero training tools or scalable content.

In both cases? The same thing happens: The field loses trust.

Field leaders talk, and what they talk about is infrastructure.

Not in those words. But in experience. They're asking: "Why does this app crash every time I try to log in?" "Why does the volume report take ninety seconds to load?" "Why can't I track what's working and what's not?" "Why is the new guy spending hours just trying to find a basic getting started video?"

This is where trust erodes. Slowly. Silently. Permanently.

If your field doesn't trust the tools, they'll create their own. Then you lose control of the message, the systems, and the duplication.

Don't obsess over creating the perfect tool. Build systems that teach people how to use the tool—then measure if they're doing it.

Some companies run by quick-fix executives get tool-happy. They launch a new app, AI voice note generator, or CRM integration every quarter—hoping technology will solve the culture problems they're afraid to address. Again, most aren't bad people—they simply haven't studied the channel long enough to know what actually works. It sounds impressive. But what's actually happening? Your average rep is overwhelmed. They don't know what to use, when to use it, or how to plug new people in.

So they freeze. Or they ghost, and suddenly you've got the illusion of innovation—but the reality of stalled duplication.

Smart infrastructure investment looks different:

A back office that loads quickly, tracks cleanly, and speaks in human terms. A tech stack that simplifies—not multiplies—what the field has to do. Clear scorecards and dashboards for reps to measure activity and rank metrics. Dynamic onboarding paths based on user behavior, not just static PDFs. AI tools used to assist—not replace—the relationship-driven parts of the profession.

Not Every Company Ships a Box. But Every Company Needs Infrastructure.

Let's make one thing clear: if you're a services company, your infrastructure requirements are a different beast. And most corporate teams don't even realize it until they're knee-deep in missed deadlines, broken systems, and field leaders asking, "Why can't anything just work?"

This chapter can't unpack every detail of those complexities — but we can give you a working lens.

Here are **three core categories of services companies** and what makes their infrastructure needs different:

1. Licensed Professional Services

Examples: financial services, real estate, insurance

- Compliance isn't a department—it's the backbone. You're managing licenses, credentials, continuing education, and state-by-state regulations that shift constantly.

- You need tracking systems, automated alerts for expirations, and airtight audit trails.

- If your infrastructure can't prove every dotted "i" and crossed "t," you're not just inefficient—you're exposed.

2. Traditional Network Marketing Services

Examples: travel, energy, wellness subscriptions, coaching platforms, software tools, education systems

- You're not delivering products—you're delivering experiences, savings, or access.

- That means partnerships, vendor APIs, booking engines, and customer service layers that aren't just nice—they're essential.

- If your tools can't confirm delivery or usage, you'll spend more time putting out fires than building belief.

Bottom Line: You can't copy-paste a product-based infrastructure and expect it to work for a service company. Different rules. Different friction points. Different risks.

The best service companies build backwards from delivery—not from design.

If you're in services and you haven't re-evaluated your tools in the last 12 months, you're overdue. What got you to launch won't get you to scale. And what you ignore now becomes what breaks you later.

And internally: Hiring based on stage, not ego. You don't need a Chief Innovation Officer before you've nailed retention. A people strategy that accounts for scale, not just titles. Knowing when to outsource vs. in-house. Budgeting not just for launch—but for post-launch support.

Over scaling breaks you.

Some companies fall into the trap of looking successful too soon. They bring on 15 employees before they've even crossed $1M in monthly revenue. They sign a lease on a 10,000 sq ft office no one asked for. They chase the appearance of growth instead of the margin for longevity.

Then one quarter turns, so they start cutting—and the field feels it. That's when the churn starts.

This isn't about being lean. It's about being smart.

Every infrastructure decision should answer this question: "How does this support trust, retention, or scalable growth?" If it doesn't? It's a vanity expense. Cut it.

AI can help you scale, but it can't replace leadership.

From content generation to onboarding bots, companies are integrating AI into nearly every piece of infrastructure. AI can help you create onboarding journeys faster, draft content for recognition campaigns, analyze rep behavior, automate basic support tasks.

But AI is not a replacement for leadership. Think of AI like electricity. It makes everything run faster — but if you wire it wrong, it will burn the house down.

Your team still needs belief. Your leaders still need strategy. Your customers still need connection.

Don't train robots. Develop people.

When you think of infrastructure built to last in direct selling, think of accountability formats, leadership progression, scorecards and income-producing activities, weekly rhythm with structured mentorship.

Your systems should promote real actions. Not just content consumption.

Don't confuse watching training with taking action. Don't mistake clicking through slides with building a business. Don't think automation replaces duplication.

You don't need more clicks. You need more conversations.

Your infrastructure should reflect your culture.

If your tools are clunky, confusing, and bloated — your field will be, too. If your tools are simple, actionable, and grounded in belief — your teams will follow suit.

Tools = framework. Humans = the building. When your infrastructure works seamlessly, you're not just building efficiency—you're building trust.

When systems work, the field feels supported. When the field feels supported, they perform.

If you're scaling without scalable infrastructure, you're not building a business built to last in direct selling. You're just buying time.

Every quarter you delay these infrastructure decisions, you're making it easier for competitors to poach your best people. They're not just taking leaders—they're taking your playbook.

The smartest move you can make isn't the flashiest. It's the one that allows your reps to plug in, perform, and repeat.

Because what you build it with is what it stands or falls—on.

Legacy companies understand something others don't: Infrastructure is culture in action.

When your systems work seamlessly, when your tools actually help instead of hinder, when your field can focus on building relationships instead of fighting technology—that's when you know you're building something that lasts.

The companies still standing in ten years won't be the ones who had the fanciest launch. They'll be the ones who built the strongest foundation.

Great infrastructure supports growth. But growth without guardrails leads to disaster. The challenge? How do you stay compliant without killing the culture that drives your success? Because most field leaders have the same reaction to compliance: 'Oh, you mean the sales prevention department?'

International expansion reveals every weakness in your foundation. But infrastructure problems don't wait for you to go global—they kill momentum at home first.

Compliance isn't the enemy. In fact, it might be the best weapon you're ignoring. While your competitors are playing compliance defense— dodging lawyers and hoping nobody notices their wild claims—you could be playing offense. Making compliance your competitive advantage. Making it the reason people trust you more, not less.

CHAPTER 12

COMPLIANCE AS COMPETITIVE ADVANTAGE

You can build the most elegant infrastructure in the world. But if compliance becomes the enemy of culture, you'll watch your best leaders walk away from everything you built.

Ask any seasoned field leader what they used to think about compliance and you'll hear the same joke: "Oh, you mean the sales prevention department?"

That's what we called it when I was building. Why? Because it felt like compliance existed just to say no. No to good promotions. No to big vision. No to momentum. To be fair, compliance should say no sometimes. But when the department loses the plot, when they operate in isolation from growth strategy, the entire company suffers.

BUILT TO LAST IN DIRECT SELLING

Through working with leaders across twenty three countries and hosting elite masterminds, you realize that the most successful companies aren't just the boldest. They're the safest. Now, many of them went through hype phases early on—that's natural in this industry. But the ones that lasted learned quickly from those mistakes and pivoted to building sustainable, long-term cultures instead of chasing the next short-term high.

This chapter isn't about knocking compliance. It's about giving corporate a new lens for it. A better framework. A smarter fusion between guardrails and community.

Your best compliance strategy is your culture.

If you want a business built to last in direct selling, you need world-class compliance. You need systems in place to keep you FTC- and FDA-compliant. You need clear language guidelines, income and product claims policies, approved materials, and documented enforcement processes.

This isn't about fear. It's about protecting the field you worked so hard to build.

But companies mess it up when they think compliance is a department. It's not. It's a culture.

You don't need your field constantly asking, "Can I say this?" or "Am I allowed to post that?" You need them to know — because you trained them well, modeled it clearly, and created an environment where doing it right actually mattered.

Patagonia proved that owning your mess builds stronger communities.

1990s. Patagonia finds out their cotton is poisoning rivers. They go public, switch to organic, and ask customers to buy less. Sales dip for two years, then explode—up 30% the next year. They donate 1% of sales, become a B Corp, and build a customer base that's loyal for life. Patagonia's "Don't Buy This Jacket" campaign becomes a legend.

Compliance isn't paperwork. It's owning your mess, fixing it in public, and inviting your community in to hold you accountable.

For direct selling, compliance isn't about checking boxes. It's about building a community that trusts you to do the right thing, even when it's hard.

AdvoCare & Vemma: The Cost of Ignoring Compliance

For years, AdvoCare was the poster child for "opportunity." Their events were packed, their products were everywhere, and their field was told they could "earn unlimited income" and "achieve financial freedom." But under the surface, the cracks were widening. AdvoCare's comp plan required heavy monthly minimums—what the field called "garage qualifying." To earn full commissions, reps had to buy $1,200–$2,400 in product up front and keep buying thousands of dollars more every year. Over 80% of product revenue came from distributor purchases, not real customers. The FTC called it "indefensible." The focus was on recruiting and buying rank, not retail sales. The company's own CEO was quoted in FTC filings as promoting the idea that anyone could "quit their job and live the dream"—but less than 5% of distributors ever earned more than $1,000 a year.

The conflict exploded in 2019. After a multi-year investigation, the FTC hit AdvoCare with a $150 million fine and banned them from MLM forever. Over 224,000 distributors lost money and received refunds from the FTC in 2025. AdvoCare's field was blindsided. Overnight, the "business opportunity" was gone. The company pivoted to retail, but the magic was lost. The brand, once a household name, became the warning label for every future comp-plan meeting.

Vemma's story followed the same script. In 2015, the FTC froze Vemma's assets and accused them of running a pyramid scheme—paying on recruitment, not product sales. Their marketing was built on income claims and recruitment hype. The court found Vemma's materials "deceptive and misleading," and the company was ordered to pay a $238 million fine and restructure its comp plan to ban recruitment-based pay. The CEO and top promoters were barred from MLM for life. The field, once thousands strong, evaporated. Vemma's successor company was forced to require real retail sales to survive. What ultimately got them in trouble was the hype-driven lifestyle promotion that drew regulatory attention.

The resolution? AdvoCare didn't vanish—but they were forced to abandon their Network Marketing model entirely. Despite having 200,000 preferred customers, according to FTC filings only 20% of revenue came from actual retail sales. They ignored years of comp plan red flags and ended up negotiating from weakness. Vemma collapsed entirely. The FTC sent a clear message: compliance isn't a department. It's the foundation.

Social media makes it worse and better.

The speed of growth on social media has only made the compliance job harder. People copy, paste, screenshot, repost, and use AI tools to spin claims faster than your legal team can keep up.

One top distributor makes a wild claim on a reel and two days later it's been reposted 137 times by people in six different countries.

Most companies go full clampdown mode. They email warnings. They take access away. They shut it all down. But it's not scalable.

What is scalable: Train the field on day one. Bake it into the onboarding. Do monthly refreshers. Create short videos and use real examples from the field. Reward the teams who model it well. Make it part of the brand.

When you create a culture where people are proud to do it right, you'll find you need fewer rules, because now the community is self-regulating.

How To Align Compliance And Culture In 3 Moves

Move 1: Train compliance like duplication—early, often, and with real examples

Don't wait until someone screws up to teach compliance.
Build it into onboarding the same way you build in product training.
Use real examples from your field—both good and bad.
Show them what *compliant* success looks like.
Make it as normal as teaching how to invite.
When compliance is part of the culture from day one, it stops feeling like rules and starts feeling like professionalism.

Move 2: Make field leaders your compliance champions—not corporate police

Your top leaders have more influence than any legal department ever will.
Train them to spot problems early.
Coach their teams on proper claims.

Model professional standards.
When field leaders *own* compliance instead of resenting it, they become your most powerful enforcement tool.
Peer pressure beats corporate pressure every time.

Move 3: Celebrate compliant behavior as professional behavior

Recognize the teams who consistently do it right.
Feature compliant content in your corporate channels.
Make following the rules feel like *leadership*, not limitation.
When you celebrate people for being professional, more people want to be professional.
Stop treating compliance like a necessary evil.
Start treating it like a competitive advantage.

The culture is your greatest safeguard.

You can't regulate your way into duplication. But you can culture your way into it.

When leaders see compliance as part of being professional, part of being a protector of their team — then you've won.

Compliance isn't the sales prevention department. It's the integrity insurance plan.

And the field? They're not your compliance enemy—they're your reputation insurance. Train them right, and they'll protect the company culture you've spent years building.

Let your culture become the best compliance tool you've ever had. Because in an era of heightened scrutiny, compliance isn't just legal protection—it's trust insurance for an entire profession.

Compliance protects what you've built. But building a culture where compliance feels natural instead of forced? That's what separates legacy companies from flash-in-the-pan failures. How you build is what you become.

Compliance without culture kills momentum. But culture without intentional infrastructure kills longevity. The companies that survive both understand a simple truth

CHAPTER 13

BUILDING FOR LEGACY

How You Build Is What You Become.

Companies that build personal development into their DNA don't just create better businesses—they create better people. Better people build legacies that outlast any product cycle or market shift. When personal growth becomes part of your company's operating system, you're not just building a business model—you're building a movement that people want to be part of for decades, not just quarters.

Infrastructure isn't "just operations." It's your strategy in disguise. It's the real test of whether you're building to scale—or just to survive another ninety days.

The companies that thrive long term in network marketing aren't always the loudest. They're not the ones shouting about AI or bragging about their latest app. They're the ones who made quiet, smart investments into the systems that matter.

They didn't confuse flash with foundation.

Network marketing isn't dying. But it's under attack by private equity vultures who treat our companies like ATMs—leveraging them with debt, cutting field support, and flipping them before the culture collapses.

This isn't a hit piece on private equity. Not all PE deals implode. Immunotec's Dynamic growth under Mauricio Domenzain with Nexxus Capital, LegalShield's successful transition from public to private company by MidOcean Partners and the subsequent addition of Stone Point Capital, and Primerica's IPO supported by Warburg Pincus—these prove it's not the involvement of PE that's the problem. It's how the astounding arrogance combined with the ignorance about how direct selling works of most PE firms can destroy enterprise value, not create it. It's the mindset that treats field relationships as transactions instead of partnerships. But what I've been seeing over and over again is a pattern that's undermining trust and weakening the foundation of companies in our space.

Let me break down what most people don't understand: the difference between venture capital and private equity. Most people lump them together, but they're different games.

Venture capital is like betting on a wild horse. You're investing early, often pre-revenue or in the very early stages. It's riskier. You help grow the company and ride the wave. The timeline is longer. The patience is built in.

Private equity is a different beast. These firms come in after the company is already established or is in distress. They usually buy a big chunk—or all—of it. They see ways to "optimize" or cut costs and create a growth story. The bigger point is less about how much they believe and more about how long they plan on staying. And spoiler alert: it's not long.

Private equity works in most industries. You buy a company, optimize operations, improve margins, sell for a profit in 3-7 years. Makes sense. It's logical. It's about numbers, optimization, margin improvements. You clean things up, improve EBITDA, sell it for a profit.

But network marketing doesn't work like most industries.

Network marketing is messy. It's emotional. It's relationship-driven. It's about belief. It's about trust. It's about leaders who've been building for years, sometimes decades. It's about new reps who need time to grow. It's about community that can't be manufactured overnight.

RODAN + FIELDS: WHEN PROMISE MET REALITY - FINAL VERSION

When TPG Capital made their minority investment in Rodan + Fields in May 2018, the timing couldn't have looked better. The skincare company had just posted $1.5 billion in 2017 revenue—a staggering 40% growth rate that made them the #1 U.S. "Premium" skincare brand. With over 200,000 consultants and 2 million customers across three countries, the momentum was undeniable.

TPG's investment valued the company at $4 billion. The promise? Leverage TPG's digital expertise and global network to fuel U.S. growth, expand internationally, and modernize the direct sales model for the social media era. The field was energized. Corporate was optimistic. Even skeptics had to admit the fundamentals looked strong.

For the first year, it looked like a win. Rodan + Fields held its leadership position through 2019. Lash Boost exploded in popularity. The company expanded into Canada and Australia. Consultant tools got a tech upgrade. Revenue hovered around $1.6 billion, and the consultant base stayed solid.

But by the end of 2019, the cracks started showing.

A 15% workforce reduction hit eighty six corporate employees. Officially it was to "eliminate inefficiencies." Unofficially, it hinted at stress below the surface.

Then came the unraveling.

CEO Diane Dietz stepped down in March 2021, after five years at the helm. Revenue had already fallen to $1.3 billion by the end of 2019, and Moody's forecasted it would dip below $1 billion by 2024. An FTC warning letter in April 2020 over COVID-related earnings claims added more heat. The company also settled a $38 million class action over alleged Lash Boost side effects.

By 2022, internal data revealed just how tough things had gotten. A law firm-led class action lawsuit that has now hit a dozen companies filed a major lawsuit in 2022 over consultant misclassification—still pending as of mid-2024.

In July 2024, the company announced it would officially exit the MLM model, effective September 1, 2024. Recruitment commissions were eliminated. One hundred corporate employees were laid off. The field was shifted to a lean affiliate program—a hard pivot from a legacy model that once drove $1.5 billion in annual sales.

This wasn't a field failure.

Consultants didn't show up because private equity placed a CEO with no channel experience. Comp plan changes and other seemingly small decisions eroded trust.

The breakdown came from the top.

Too many pivots. Too little vision. Not enough listening.

When companies optimize for quarters instead of decades—this is how it ends.

When companies look at the salesforce as transactional vs people, it's the beginning of the end.

How you build is what you become. And in a profession working to rebuild its reputation, every infrastructure decision either builds credibility or destroys it. Build accordingly.

You can build with legacy in mind. You can create systems that outlast you. But legacy means nothing if it dies the moment you step away.

CHAPTER 14

THE LEGACY PLAY

If you're not building something bigger than you, you're building something that dies with you.

In the early days of this profession, legacy was the vision. Not just the products. Not just the comp plans. But the dream.

They'd talk about creating something you could pass on. Not just income. Memories. Impact. Time freedom.

You'd hear things like: "Take one year to learn it… Three years to make a full-time income… Five to make a big income… Seven to create something world-class."

Now, were those numbers guaranteed? Of course not. But they cast vision. They gave people something to fight for. To build toward. To believe in.

And belief—not hype—is what creates legacy.

We've lost the long game.

The Trust Recession Timeline:
How We Lost the Long Game

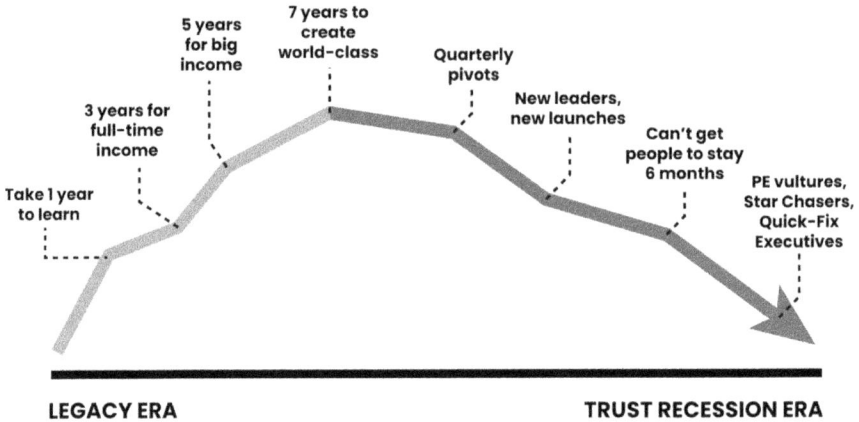

Take 1 year to learn

3 years for full-time income

5 years for big income

7 years to create world-class

Quarterly pivots

New leaders, new launches

Can't get people to stay 6 months

PE vultures, Star Chasers, Quick-Fix Executives

LEGACY ERA

TRUST RECESSION ERA

**We used to tell people this was worth giving years to.
Now we can't get them to stay for months.**

Now, it's all quarterly pivots. New leaders. New launches. New distractions. Corporate blames the field, and the field blames corporate.

Both sides have gotten away from the basics while three enemies attack our profession: Private equity vultures leveraging companies to death, star hunting executives creating revolving doors, and quick-fix executives slapping promos over real problems. We used to tell people this was a business worth giving years to. Now we can't even get people to stay for six months. Yet we wonder why no one trusts the model anymore.

Legacy companies don't play to survive. They play to endure.

They stick to long-term strategy, not short-term sprints. Train for depth, not just firepower. Build with the next generation in mind.

Reinforce systems until they duplicate. Invest in people—not just platforms.

And they build for more than themselves. Because legacy isn't something you own, it's something you leave behind.

If you're in corporate, let this land.

You used to cast a vision that got people to dream again. Not just sell. You talked about family, time, and purpose. Now too many talk about growth hacks, influencer funnels, and conversion rates.

There's nothing wrong with tools. But people didn't join to build a funnel, they joined to build a life.

Ask yourself: Would your best leaders stay five years if they never hit the top rank? If the honest answer is no, you're not building a legacy— you're running a high-end recruiting scheme.

Legacy doesn't mean stale—it means stable.

It doesn't mean slow—it means sustainable.

Nobody wants to say this out loud: You will never create a movement if people are only here for themselves. Legacy happens when they believe they're part of something bigger.

You can't just tell them that. You have to show it—in how you build.

What legacy looks like today:

Promoting people, not just paychecks. Training on consistency, not just charisma. Designing systems that last longer than your CMO. Building communities that outlive leaders built to last in direct selling.

It's not about becoming the biggest. It's about becoming the most trusted. Because ultimately, that's what people are really looking for.

Bring back the vision.

Bring back the belief in building something worth staying for. Stop playing "Who can launch the fastest?" and start asking "Who's still going to be here in ten years?"

The legacy play isn't hype. It's not trendy. It's not even flashy. But it's the only thing that actually builds trust, and it's the only thing worth chasing.

Not just for you. But for the people who will come after you.

This profession was never supposed to be about hype, shortcuts, or chasing stars. It was always about people — about belief, duplication, and building something that lasts.

What started as an idea to bridge trust between corporate and field leaders turned into something bigger. A handbook. A lens. A callout. A reset.

If we've done our job right, this isn't the end of the conversation. It's the beginning.

If you're corporate, this is your invitation to step up as a partner — not a puppet master. To be the standard for retention, for leadership development, for meaningful culture. You don't have to be perfect. You just have to be in the fight for the right reasons.

If you're in the field, this is your reminder that no company or comp plan will ever outwork belief, consistency, and leadership. The best systems still require someone to pick up the key, turn the lock, and lead others through the door.

We've covered everything from launch strategy to leadership ascension. From recognition to infrastructure. From tools to trust. It all matters. It all plays a role.

But in the end, what will matter most is this:

Did you build something people want to be part of?
Did you create a brand that matches your values?
Did you cast vision that outlives your paycheck?

This is the Trust Recession era. But the good news is, trust can be rebuilt. And if you do it right, you won't just grow a company — you'll lead a movement.

The kind people want to stay with. The kind people want to fight for. The kind that becomes your legacy. Because the real legacy isn't just what you build—it's how you help restore trust in an entire profession.

Building for legacy requires long-term thinking. But legacy isn't automatic—it's intentional. And if you're not building something bigger than you, you're building something that dies with you.

The real legacy isn't just what you build—it's who you help people become while building it. Because eventually, products become obsolete, comp plans get restructured, and companies get sold. But the person someone becomes through personal development? That's theirs forever—and that's the legacy worth fighting for.

You've seen the frameworks.

The field-tested systems.

The behind-the-scenes truths.

CHAPTER 15

LOCK IT IN – FROM INSIGHT TO IMPLEMENTATION

Now what?

Most execs will finish a book like this, feel inspired for a couple days, then go right back to playing corporate whack-a-mole. Budget reviews. Launch meetings. Another internal memo that sounds good but goes nowhere.

That's how companies lose momentum.

The ones that win long-term aren't chasing the flashiest new idea. They're the ones that *implement*. The ones that *fix the leaks*. The ones that do the boring stuff really well—over and over again.

Implementation isn't sexy—it's necessary.

Next week, your CMO will pitch a new tool. Someone will suggest an AI idea that confuses your field even more. Your leadership team will start talking about the next incentive trip—before the last one even paid out properly.

You'll be tempted to chase novelty instead of reinforcing what actually drives growth.

Don't.

The companies that are built to last?

- Don't confuse apps for strategy.

- Don't outsource field trust to marketing teams.

- Don't wait for the field to burn out before asking what they need.

What Implementation Looks Like

Start small. Choose one thing from this book. Not five.

If retention is broken, install the Four-Month Loyalty Lock System and track it for ninety days.

If your team is burnt out trying to build leaders from scratch, roll out the Leadership Ascension Ladder.

If events are just feel-good weekends with no follow-up, implement the 5 Event Non-Negotiables and build an actual momentum window.

Do it completely. Measure it. Then move on to the next.

The Real Decision

You've got two options now.

You can close this book, tell your team it was "a good read," and go right back to running your business the same way.

Or you can use this as a blueprint. Not theory. Not hype. Just honest systems that work—if you do.

This profession doesn't need more slogans. It needs infrastructure. Leadership. Culture people can believe in again.

Why I Wrote This

I've seen it from both sides.

Stuart Johnson, founder and CEO of Direct Selling News, challenged me to write this book. He saw something I didn't—that having built in the field and consulted behind the scenes gave me a unique perspective this profession needed. Stuart was right. Someone needs to bridge the gap between corporate strategy and field reality.

I've built at the top of the field. I've spoken in twenty three countries. I've trained thousands of six and seven-figure earners, and now I consult behind the scenes—helping owners and executive teams shift from short-term noise to long-term trust.

That's rare in this profession—someone who can speak *both languages*.

This book isn't about what looks good on a slide. It's about what actually lasts after the next comp plan tweak, leadership exit, or social media trend.

Let's build something the field actually wants to fight for.

– Rob

THE REAL LEGACY IS WHAT YOU BUILD WHEN NO ONE'S WATCHING

The Momentum Sustainability Test

Will Your Company Still Be Growing in 5 Years?

The most dangerous position in network marketing isn't being small—it's being flat.

A $5M company growing to $7M attracts leaders like a magnet. A $100M company dropping to $95M repels them like poison. Momentum is about catching tailwinds, not rowing harder into headwinds. Every team can grind through challenges—but smart companies leverage timing and culture like a sail.

People don't join momentum—they join the story of momentum. That story is either "we're building something bigger" or "we're trying not to lose what we have."

Even though we teach people that network marketing isn't a lottery ticket, they're still hoping to jump on a bandwagon with unstoppable momentum. That's human nature. That's why progress matters more than size, and why vision is more powerful than current reality.

The question isn't how big you are. The question is: Are you positioned for sustained progress, or are you one flat quarter away from being labeled 'declining'?

This assessment measures your company's ability to sustain forward momentum regardless of market conditions, competitive pressure, or internal challenges. Rate each area honestly. Your future relevance depends on it.

Section 1: Leadership Presence

Are you visible when momentum stalls?

Rate each statement 1-10 (1 = completely false, 10 = completely true):

__Your field knows exactly who's steering the company during crisis
__Leadership communicates vision beyond quarterly metrics
__You're present on platforms where your field actually lives
__Your leaders hear from you directly, not through middle management
__You cast 10-year vision, not just 90-day goals

Leadership Presence Score: ___/50

Momentum Assessment:

- **40-50:** Momentum-sustaining. Your presence creates confidence.

- **25-39:** Momentum-vulnerable. Silence creates doubt about direction.

- **Below 25:** Momentum-killing. Your absence suggests decline.

Section 2: The Culture Cancer Test

How momentum-resistant is your culture?

Rate each statement 1-10:

___Recognition isn't just reserved for top 1% performers
___Your stated values match your actual decisions under pressure
___Field leaders feel safe giving honest feedback without retaliation
___Mid-level builders feel empowered, not overlooked
___You protect culture from toxic high producers

Culture Cancer Score: ___/50

Momentum Assessment:

- **40-50:** Momentum-building. Strong culture accelerates growth.

- **25-39:** Momentum-dragging. Cultural gaps slow progress.

- **Below 25:** Momentum-destroying. Toxic culture kills forward motion.

Section 3: The Compensation Collapse Predictor

Is your comp plan momentum-sustaining or momentum-killing?

Rate each statement 1-10:

___Your plan rewards behavior, not just outcomes
___Payouts are sustainable even during volume dips
___New reps can earn meaningful money in first 90 days
___You're not paying advances just to recruit leaders
___Your plan creates loyalty, not just hype

Compensation Collapse Score: ___/50

Momentum Assessment:

- **40-50:** Momentum-sustaining. Built for consistent progress.

- **25-39:** Momentum-unstable. Cracks forming under pressure.

- **Below 25:** Momentum-collapsing. Unsustainable trajectory.

Section 4: The Leaky Bucket Diagnostic

Is your retention sustaining or killing momentum?

Rate each statement 1-10:

___You engineer customer retention, not hope for it
___Your customer retention rate improves year-over-year
___Your top 20% earners have increasing tenure vs. decreasing
___You track what makes customers choose to stay vs. leave
___Retention is owned by corporate, not outsourced to field
___Your field genuinely uses and loves your products personally
___Customers reorder because of results, not just relationships

Leaky Bucket Score: ___/70

Momentum Assessment:

- **40-50:** Momentum-building. Your bucket holds progress.

- **25-39:** Momentum-slowing. Leaks are holding you back.

- **Below 25:** Momentum-reversing. More going out than coming in.

Section 5: Event Integrity

Do your events build momentum or kill it?

Rate each statement 1-10:

___Your events create emotional connection, not just information transfer
___Field leaders help plan agendas, not just attend them
___You don't stream your main event (making attendance optional)
___Recognition reflects reality, not just elite status
___People leave believing more than when they arrived

Event Integrity Score: ___/50

MOMENTUM ASSESSMENT:

- **40-50:** Momentum-multiplying. Events accelerate belief.

- **25-39:** Momentum-neutral. Events feel corporate, not inspiring.

- **Below 25:** Momentum-damaging. Events actually decrease belief.

Section 6: International Commitment

Is international expansion building or killing momentum?

Rate each statement 1-10:
___You have in-country general managers with decision-making authority
___International launches are fully resourced, not drive-by experiments
___You adapt products/comp plans to local markets vs. copy-paste
___International markets trust your long-term commitment
___You invest in relationships, not just revenue extraction

International Commitment Score: ___/50

MOMENTUM ASSESSMENT:

- **60-70:** Momentum-building. International success fuels domestic growth.

- **45-59:** Momentum-neutral. International doesn't help or hurt.

- **Below 44:** Momentum-damaging. Failed launches hurt your reputation.

Section 7: Infrastructure Integrity

Does your infrastructure accelerate or slow momentum?

Rate each statement 1-10:

___Your tech stack simplifies duplication vs. complicating it
___New reps ARE successfully using your systems within their first week
___You invest in supporting what works vs. replacing what's fixable
___Field leaders trust your tools to support their growth
___Infrastructure decisions prioritize user experience over corporate convenience

Infrastructure Integrity Score: ___/50

Momentum Assessment:

- **40-50:** Momentum-accelerating. Tools amplify human progress.

- **25-39:** Momentum-slowing. Technology creates friction.

- **Below 25:** Momentum-blocking. Systems prevent progress.

Section 8: Compliance Culture

Does compliance support or slow momentum?

Rate each statement 1-10:

___Compliance is built into culture, not policed from outside
___Field leaders understand and teach compliance as professionalism
___Your compliance strategy prevents problems vs. just reacting to them
___You train compliance like you train duplication—often and well
___Compliance protects momentum, it doesn't restrict it

Compliance Culture Score: ___/50

Momentum Assessment:

- **40-50:** Momentum-protecting. Compliance enables sustainable growth.

- **25-39:** Momentum-slowing. Compliance feels restrictive.

- **Below 25:** Momentum-stopping. Compliance blocks progress.

Section 9: The Leader Factory Blueprint

Are you building momentum through leadership development?

Rate each statement 1-10:

___You develop leaders internally vs. poaching from competitors
___Leadership advancement is earned through proven systems vs. purchased with deals
___You have clear pathways from new rep to top leadership
___Your leaders aren't looking elsewhere because they believe in your company's future ___Development investments create loyalty, not just skills

Leader Factory Score: ___/50

MOMENTUM ASSESSMENT:

- **40-50:** Momentum-building. Growing your own leadership bench.

- **25-39:** Momentum-dependent. Relying too heavily on external recruitment.

- **Below 25:** Momentum-killing. Leadership gaps slow everything down.

Section 10: Legacy Mindset

Are you building sustainable momentum or short-term spikes?

Rate each statement 1-10:

___Decisions are made with 5-year consequences in mind
___You'd rather build consistently than spike and crash
___Short-term profits don't override long-term momentum
___Your field believes this company's best days are ahead
___You're building something that gets stronger over time

Legacy Mindset Score: ___/50

Momentum Assessment:

- **40-50:** Momentum-sustaining. Building for decades, not quarters.

- **25-39:** Momentum-vulnerable. Short-term thinking threatens progress.

- **Below 25:** Momentum-unsustainable. Operating in survival mode.

Total Momentum Sustainability Score: ___/520

Overall Momentum Assessment:

400-520: MOMENTUM SUSTAINABLE Your company is positioned for sustained growth regardless of market conditions. You've built momentum that compounds over time rather than requiring constant fuel.

300-399: MOMENTUM VULNERABLE You have significant gaps that threaten sustained progress. Focus immediately on your three lowest-scoring areas before they kill your forward motion.

200-299: MOMENTUM ENDANGERED Your momentum is fragile and could stall at any time. Multiple vulnerabilities make sustained growth unlikely without major improvements.

Below 200: MOMENTUM FAILING Your company is already losing momentum, whether you see it or not. Every quarter you delay addressing these gaps makes recovery harder and relevance more distant.

THE REALITY: No assessment can guarantee perpetual growth. Markets shift, leaders make unexpected decisions, and external factors impact every company. However, companies that score high on this assessment dramatically increase their probability of sustained momentum regardless of circumstances.

In an industry where direction matters more than size, momentum isn't luck—it's the result of intentional systems that compound progress over time. From your infrastructure to your international strategy, from compliance to leadership development—every system either accelerates belief or erodes it.

The choice is yours: Build momentum that lasts, or become another company that used to matter.

ABOUT THE AUTHOR

Rob Sperry has spent two decades in the direct selling profession—coaching, consulting, and building alongside the top one percent of earners and executives. He's personally trained over 1,700 verified six and seven-figure earners inside his private masterminds. His podcast has been downloaded in 176 countries. He's spoken in twenty three countries, hosted over thirty elite leadership events, and served as a strategic advisor to some of the industry's most innovative and legacy companies.

Rob is the author of eighteen books and known for helping top field leaders scale with systems, not just hype. His content isn't fluff—it's rooted in what actually duplicates in today's market. Through his high-level consulting and training platforms, he bridges the gap between corporate strategy and field execution.

When he's not consulting or coaching, you'll find him with his family, coaching High School tennis, or helping youth through personal development events every month.

www.ingramcontent.com/pod-product-compliance
Ingram Content Group UK Ltd.
Pitfield, Milton Keynes, MK11 3LW, UK
UKHW020131091025
463744UK00012B/176

9 798990 398894